To

C000175643

LIFTING THE VEILS OF ILLUSION

Stay magical +
shine on !

Love + Light

Narina xx

There is a rainbow in the sky;
a symbol of hope;
a favourable omen

There's a rainbow in a dewdrop;
as above so below

There's a rainbow in your body,
an array of energy—
often called the chakras

The rainbow is a bridge
to outlandish dimensions
that you often frequent

LIFTING THE VEILS OF ILLUSION

7 STEPS TOWARDS SPIRITUAL ENLIGHTENMENT

BY
NARINA RISKOWITZ

Practical Inspiration
PUBLISHING

First published in Great Britain by Practical Inspiration Publishing.

ISBN (print): 978-1-910056-38-7
ISBN (ebook): 978-1-910056-39-4

For more information,
see www.liftingtheveilsofillusion.co.uk

This book is dedicated to everyone who has and will be attending my transformational workshops, courses and one-to-one sessions. I am immensely grateful to you. I am on this journey with you, and because of you.

Acknowledgements

With thanks to Alison Jones of Practical Inspiration Publishing, for your professional assistance and positive encouragement.

Also to my soul family for your heart-warming stories, reflections and poems. Your contributions and ongoing support make this journey a joy.

Finally, thanks to my many teachers. I learn from everyone I come in contact with. Many of you are sent to assist me on this journey, and you make it a magical one.

Table of Contents

APPENDIX 4

Preface

Warning!

The concepts in this book might change your life. At first it may seem that they can't be true, as we resist them with all our might. As you contemplate them more, they begin to shake up your model of the world in a way that sets in motion a life-altering process. Although challenging at first, this process will be altogether good for you. You'll begin to take charge of your life. You'll also be guided in this process, and as you follow it through, more and more light and joy will shine through until you begin to experience the outcomes you always wanted in your life.

Another Warning!

This book contains powerful transformational techniques. Although transformation is essentially healing, and will change your life for the better, it may be accompanied by challenging growing pains. These pains will only exist if you hang onto your old model of the world for dear life, as I used to. Transformation is a radical change of form, such as a caterpillar becoming a butterfly. A butterfly, as you know, is magnificent. What you might not know is that to achieve this magnificent new form, the pupa in the chrysalis becomes liquid. It goes through a complete meltdown! Although not always comfortable, transformation will be altogether good for you. When you flow with the change, it is always easier to accept.

Oh, Another Warning!

There is no way back. Oh dear. Well, at least you've been warned. Once you lift the veils of illusion and begin to see life for what it is, you can't go back to the seemingly comfortable old. It will be as if you are in a whole new dimension with different, even paradoxical, laws. Fortunately, new dimensions present new opportunities. So again, it will be altogether good for you.

This path has been trodden by many before, and these people have left wisdom and guidelines for us to follow. One such person was Carl Jung, the psychologist. Jung opened us up to the magic of the unconscious mind and what he called the collective unconscious mind. These are the realms, now uncovered in quantum physics as well, that we will be exploring in this book. To access them, we will lift the veils of illusion that have kept us from seeing a reality so magical, it's no wonder it's been veiled in confusion, disbelief, illusion and secrecy. Fortunately we have grown and matured to a level where we are ready to lift these veils, take a peek into the unseen and face a magical reality, very different from the one in which we've grown up.

Introduction

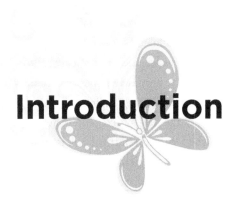

Welcome to this journey of personal development and spiritual growth.

Although the path is different for everyone, each of us must climb essential steps to reach the next level of growth and awareness. Every step contains valuable lessons and experiences, which are always incorporated into the next level of understanding, so we cannot skip a step.

During this journey we will lift the veils of illusion, share ancient wisdom and undergo powerful transformational processes.

The 7 Steps process is designed to provide useful insights and serve as a guide on your path towards development, growth and enlightenment.

This process is unique in that not only is it informative, interactive and experiential, it is also hugely transformational. You will experience personal transformation as you release the patterns of the past and will be left with a clean slate on which you can write your own purpose in your own way.

You will experience healing and accelerated growth. You will feel ready and prepared to enter a new era of enlightenment.

We are so privileged to live in this unique transitional time in the evolution of humankind. An unparalleled shift in energy and consciousness is affecting our level of awareness dramatically, allowing us to see everything in a whole new light. Many people are now waking up to who they truly are, remembering their true purpose. We are living in a time of mass awakening unlike any other. The changes are happening quickly. The intention of this book is to shed light on the process in the context of this magical time we live in, and to provide guidance and insight that will facilitate your personal and spiritual evolution.

What is expanded consciousness?

Expanding your awareness to include more of what is going on around you, physically, mentally and emotionally. Through expanded consciousness, we bring more and more of the unconscious into conscious awareness; we become aware of the subtle synchronicity in life and the interconnectedness of everything. Through expanded consciousness, the veils of illusion lift and we can see what's real.

What is awakening?

Waking up to the fact that you are spirit in human experience. Awakening is a shift in consciousness from thinking to (present moment) awareness.

What is ascension?

Raising the consciousness to higher frequencies of energy vibration. It involves drawing down light into the body and raising your energy vibrations to become a higher being of light and energy.

What is enlightenment?

Seeing clearly. For the Buddhist, enlightenment is having wisdom, insight and knowledge in regards to the true nature of things. The 'light comes on' and then you are filled with light. To see clearly, we have to see through the illusions. On the journey through this book we aim to lift the veils of illusion so we can see clearly.

What are the veils of illusion?

Illusionary perceptions that veil the true reality from us. Buddha taught that this world is an illusion. Living in this three-dimensional world, we experience limited understanding and illusionary perceptions of the ego mind. The illusionary world of the ego, which is invested in self-importance and protection, is separated by the thinnest of veils from true reality; in the same way, the three-dimensional world is separated from the fourth- and fifth-dimensional worlds by the thinnest of veils. As we awaken and grow in consciousness, we begin to see through the illusions. During this journey we will explore these illusions. Each of the 7 steps will lift another veil of illusion. When a veil is lifted, you will find yourself in a whole new plane of existence, perceiving everything very differently than before. Looking back you will realize how you've changed, and this is the magic of transformation.

Describing the Journey

The 7 Steps journey is designed to take you through a process. Some concepts may be familiar, in which case, take the opportunity to review the essential foundational principles and perhaps gain a different perspective. The first step is fundamental, and we revisit it often. The journey is a process of self-discovery – discovering who you truly are and what you are capable of. The concepts and processes in this book are powerful, transformational and designed to bring about shifts towards higher levels of consciousness.

The energy centres, or chakras, in the body effectively symbolize our personal growth and development journey through life, so I will refer to these seven energy centres to illustrate various stages of this journey. The 7 Steps journey is therefore also a journey of growth through the seven chakras. The journey of growth and development through the chakras is described in Appendix 2.

I will also refer to various stages of spiritual awakening. Each one is essential, so it's best to embrace each stage as you grow and evolve towards the next one. The journey is ongoing. There is always more to learn and new ways to perceive life as it unfolds. For example, there was a time when we thought the Earth was flat. That was just our collective level of awareness at the time. There was also a time when Einstein said that nothing would ever move faster than the speed of light. Well, recently, scientists have discovered that particles can indeed communicate faster than light, taking global society to yet another level of awareness[1]. The truth as it is perceived at the moment will only last until new discoveries and insights change our current level of awareness. Whenever this happens, a whole new world opens up to us – a different dimension of existence.

We will also look at the planes or dimensions of our existence. By now you may have noticed the magic number seven in everything. There are seven colours in the rainbow, and these colours of various vibrations are the different dimensions in which we already exist. Throughout the 7 Steps process we raise our conscious awareness to grasp and take in more light on the path to enlightenment.

The journey is inevitable. Sometimes we simply stumble upon it. Sometimes it is like navigating a maze. The 7 Steps process can serve as your guide and clarify, ease and accelerate the journey for you. So, enjoy it, your journey, as you grow in insight and evolve in life.

---

1. Talbot, 1991 and *http://www.nature.com/news/2008/080813/full/news.2008.1038.html*

Carole's Journey

Carole first came to see me experiencing stress, difficulty sleeping, aches in her lower back and low self-esteem. She was off work. Desperate to get better so that she could resume her duties, she thought of taking an alternative approach. A friend had recommended transformational therapy. She arrived somewhat anxious, not knowing what to expect. Tearfully she described her story. It was as though her whole life was falling apart. She was in a high-pressure job that she didn't enjoy; her father-in-law had just passed away; her ailing mom needed care. Her son was displaying behavioural problems at school; finances were tight; and with a leaking roof, the house needed attention.

She explained how she'd always felt odd as a child and had been bullied at school. Keen to make friends and feel accepted, she often ended up in the 'wrong' crowd. From a young age she concerned herself with what people might be thinking. As an adult in the workplace she became a people pleaser, taking on more tasks and working longer hours. This exhausting, self-perpetuating cycle started to affect her relationship with her partner. In spite of all her efforts, she was overlooked for promotion. We started exploring her choices. The mention of a job change caused her visible anxiety. 'Carole', I asked, 'if you could do anything, what would you want to do?' The answer didn't come immediately; she felt frustrated and resistant to change. Then she said, 'I've always wanted to work with children and organize events.' I encouraged her to start visualizing herself doing that. She resisted at first: 'How will I afford it? I need a fixed monthly income'.

The therapeutic process Carole followed is the process described in the pages of this book. As we worked to release fear and self-doubt, Carole's spark and natural confidence began to shine through. As soon as she had clarity on what she wanted to do, opportunities started to come her way. Within days she was approached by a children's charity that needed an event organizer. The experience she gained with the charity was invaluable and made up for the initial drop in income. She felt happy and encouraged to follow her dream.

We live in a time right now, where people and circumstances that don't serve you any longer will drop away, if you allow them to. Carole's story is just one of many that reflects this clearly. This life-changing process can sometimes go hand in hand with great discomfort initially. Ultimately it leads to the happy life that's been there waiting for you.

Jenny's Journey

Jenny was experiencing what she described as severe anxiety and depression, a common phenomenon these days. Exhausted, she felt that the anxiety was getting out of control and leading to insomnia. She carried long-held emotions and negative thinking patterns from childhood. Her marriage was breaking down. Previous relationships had been unhappy experiences. At one time, she had been left for another woman, and she feared it might happen again.

We started by releasing the old anger and sadness, and Jenny began to brighten up. When we began to release fear and a history of self-doubt, the change in her was incredible. Her energy returned, and with that, her inner strength and her joy for life. She started to feel like her old confident self again and began to realize her true worth. Finally able to let go of her past and all the unnecessary baggage she had carried around for such a long time, she felt lighter, free of cares and stress, buzzing with energy. People around her commented on how she had changed, how she looked radiant and years younger. Her future began to open up. She was able to contemplate change and future plans that previously felt scary. She had always wanted to travel, she said. She began to open up spiritually; she felt she had a specific purpose and was ready to begin exploring that purpose and sharing her unique service with the world.

Joe's Journey

When I first met Joe, he had been made redundant from a sales job. His confidence had taken a knock, and he came for interview coaching and confidence building. He felt pressured to apply for another job and achieve success as he was in a relationship that he really wanted to work. The more he wanted to please his girlfriend, the more critical she became. He felt his whole life was being challenged, and he just wanted to be happy and successful. As we began to work together, I saw so much potential in him. Joe had a keen interest in people and was fascinated by my work. We explored the difference between a job and a meaningful career. I said to Joe, 'If you could start again, what would you ideally do?' He replied, 'I've always been interested in psychology, and that's what I always seem to read about'. As we worked on recovering his confidence, I noticed that Joe also had a keen business mind – he was a true entrepreneur. As Joe grew in confidence, his idea of an ideal job began to change. Through the coaching process, he began to tap into his true potential and consider his future in a whole new way.

My Own Journey of Growth and Discovery

I too found myself unhappy in a job at one time. I began to question what I was doing and what I wanted to do. During my twenty years in public relations and communications, I'd been convinced I was on the right career path, but now I was starting to think that perhaps it was time to study something new. This might have been my midlife crisis! I took an interest in neurolinguistic programming (NLP) from a communications perspective. Unexpectedly, it opened me up to a world of personal development and transformational therapy. Midforties, I made a radical career change. Now I know that my whole life had been steering me in this direction. NLP exposed me to the field of energy, and I wanted to know more. To explore energy further, I learnt reiki, tai chi and chi kung, all of which set me on a path of energy healing.

I now know it's best to flow with change. That's how you are guided down a path that may seem strange at first – a path that's absolutely right for you. You may end up doing something you never thought you would, yet it was your calling all along. Your own journey is always your greatest teacher. As an NLP trainer, I value the NLP principles on the power of the mind, and my writings reflect these empowering NLP beliefs.

My journey inevitably ventured into the magic of Jungian and esoteric psychology. I am particularly motivated by Carl Jung's teachings on the unconscious mind and the collective unconscious. Jung is a great teacher of esoteric spirituality. All this wonderfully culminated in my work as a transformational therapist and soul coach. I studied and utilized many systems, such as the chakras, the Qabala and others that clearly describe a path of growth and development. I became fascinated with the common elements of these systems. I am inspired by great teachers who have done the same, including Deepak Chopra, Caroline Myss, my NLP teachers and my tai chi teachers; people who take personal development into spirituality and healing into the subtle realms of energy. As a result of this exposure and my work with individuals and groups, I developed the 7 Steps Course In Spiritual Growth and Enlightenment; the seven-week meditation course Lifting the Veils of Illusion; and the signature 7 Steps soul-coaching programme: Lifting the Veils of Illusion. Finally, years of tested and treasured course material resulted in this book. A journey that's ancient is now set in the new age, where it takes on current significance.

The fact that you're holding this book in your hands is no coincidence; it means you are ready to make the shift – to release the past and heal, to overcome unnecessary fears and doubts and open up as a magical creator of your life while co-creating the new Earth.

Unintended Journey

You fell off a cliff
and as you were falling
your feet tried to walk
back up again
thinking they could defy
gravity.

But gravity cannot be defied
and so you fell.

You fell in love
and as you were
falling
your heart began
to run.

Run
run
run
for your life

Your heart knows
what it is doing.

By Andrea Nolan
Ontological Leadership Coach and Inspirational Poet

Step 1: Taking Full Responsibility

Illusion 1	I live in a world of circumstances I am a victim of random circumstances I am affected by people and circumstances
Reality	You live in a world of experience created through your own thinking Your choices and thoughts create your outcomes Thoughts create emotions with vibrations that attract likeness to you You perceive the world not as it is, but as you are You can only achieve what you believe you can Any perceived limitation is self-imposed All your experiences are on the inside; they only appear to be on the outside The inner creates the outer
Shift	Make essential mental shifts from effect to cause; victim to creator Take full responsibility for everything happening in your life Become the co-creator of your life Take 100 percent responsibility because it is 100 percent empowering
Mindfulness Meditation	Reflect mindfully on thoughts, beliefs and perceptions

Our Illusionary World

As we go through life, most of us have certain routines, doing what life expects of us. We have roles and responsibilities within our families, companies, businesses and groups. We go about trying to please many people, do well in exams, excel in sport, achieve in business and career, reach a certain status and earn a living. Maybe it's a survival game: *I have to hang onto my job to earn money. I have to play it safe. I have to work harder. What's the reward? Where's the fun? Perhaps there's a holiday I can save up for. Or shall I just put it on the credit card and pay it off? Everybody does. Perhaps I can work for a grand house, a fancy car. Everybody does. How do I shape up? Perhaps I have to work harder, longer hours. How do I compare? What do others think of me?*

In its illusionary world, the ego compares, competes, struggles; it's hardly ever satisfied. It often feels like a victim of random circumstances. *Why me? Life is unfair.* The ego may even think, *Hang on, I'm in charge here. I'm clever and I'm working towards wealth, a grand house and success.*

Perhaps you have achieved great success, done it all, seen it all, got all the T-shirts – now what? Disillusioned with life, you may be wondering: *Is this it? What next? There must be more to life than this? What's real?*

For many, life in the fast lane is becoming increasingly challenging. Workloads rise, overtime hours stretch, email inboxes fill to the brim, all on top of family and home-life demands. We are constantly on the go. Never a moment to ourselves, to enjoy an interest, to exercise, let alone relax! As our lives get more and more out of balance, we feel stressed out, drained and tired. The irony is, this state of tension makes us less effective at what we do. And obviously, it takes the joy out of it. We become so focused in our tunnel vision that we lose a broader awareness. This is the small and limiting world of the ego self. Separated from it, by the thinnest of veils, is the altogether magical world of your true self.

The world that you live in, that you are conscious of in your everyday waking state, the world of form, that you can see and touch, the world of your ego mind, as real as it may seem, is a small part of who you are. Compared to an ocean, it's only a wave. It may be a magnificent wave, full of colour, beauty, might and force as it roars out across the ocean, but as a wave, it is quite aware of itself. It may look across the ocean at other waves. *Who's the strongest wave? Who's going to go the furthest? How do I compare to the other waves? What do I look like? How do I perform? What do those other waves think of me? Let's see, which wave is the mightiest and will go the furthest? I'll put on a greater show as I roll out towards the shore.* The wave's doubts and fears begin to kick in: *I want to look the best and get there first. What if I run out of steam? I better keep going! What if I collapse in the sea and become nothing?*

Inevitably the wave will collapse in the ocean. For the ego, this is death. *I'm going to die! I'll be nothing!* But then the wave realizes: *Hang on, I'm not dying. I'm held by something much bigger than me. I'm held by the ocean. This ocean is part of me. I'm not just a wave – I am the ocean.* The illusion collapses; the veil is pierced. Our wave is free to rest, to merge with the ocean. As it relaxes and sinks deeper, it becomes calm and still. The old doubts and fears are gone. It feels good. It can be creative. As it sinks deeper still and explores greater depths, it discovers great treasures below – gifts and talents that had been there all along. Because the ocean is infinite, what our wave can tap into, explore and unleash is infinite and unlimited. This is the magical world of the ocean, a wealth of inspiration and wisdom. It is peaceful and blissful. *I can just be myself – my true, magical self. It is liberating. The struggle is over. The stress and hard work is gone. Instead, I can be infinitely creative. I can expand and be fulfilled. There is so much more to explore. I can evolve. I feel joy and love. Here below, I know what's right for me. I know who I truly am and what I'm capable of.*

I have come home – to myself. I am aware of so much more. I am more of who I am. My natural, built-in confidence has returned. I don't have to be like others to feel confident. I can just be who I am. I can embrace my uniqueness. And yet, the ocean is vast and there is infinitely more to experience and become.

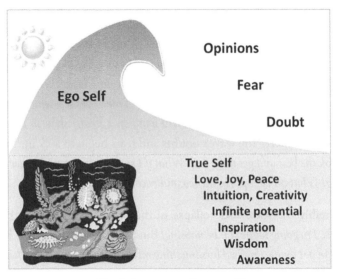

'Am I the wave or the ocean?'

First Awakening

The first awakening takes a huge mental shift; a shift in awareness. When we first awaken to our role and our personal power, everything changes. Our perceptions, beliefs, values, attitudes and approach to life change radically. The world of form becomes less solid. We become less externally orientated. Instead of looking outside ourselves for reasons why certain things are happening in our lives, we become aware of how we cause or create the events and circumstance in our lives with our thoughts, perceptions, beliefs and intentions. Empowered, we become the creators of our lives and begin to live magically. It is a huge process of self-discovery through which we come to see everything differently. The old ways are gone for good. We become aware and awake, conscious of our actions and ready to take full responsibility for our lives.

Until this first awakening we are basically spiritually asleep; unaware of the higher truth of who we really are. Consequently, as we experience life's challenges, we often feel the *effects* of people and circumstances. We then tend to point fingers and blame others, looking for excuses; for reasons outside ourselves for the mishaps in our own lives. Effectively we declare ourselves victims in an unfair world. *Victim* may sound like a harsh word here, but that's what we are whenever we feel something is happening *to* us and that we can't do anything about it. The problem with being a victim of the *effect* is that we become helpless. We feel unable to act – we become helpless victims looking for someone or something to blame to take the pressure off ourselves. It may take the pressure off temporarily but will leave us disempowered.

It's a huge mental shift, from this cosy yet powerless position to that of taking full responsibility. Shifting from victimhood to 100 percent responsibility is the first step in spiritual awakening. It is an awakening to the fact that we are essentially creators.

Thoughts Matter As They Become Matter

With our thoughts and feelings we create our own realities. Thoughts create emotions with vibrations that attract likeness to us. For example, if I perceive the world as a fearful place, I am likely to attract circumstances to me that create more fear. If I believe that people can't be trusted, I am likely to attract to me people who can't be trusted. And so, I prove myself right. It is the simple law of cause and effect. The belief attracts and creates the reality. We attract to us according to how we are. The inner creates the outer. All experiences are on the inside. Through our perceptions, experiences only appear to be external. This is why, throughout our 7 Steps journey, we continuously endeavour to bring our often subtle unconscious beliefs, perceptions and feelings into conscious awareness. Mere awareness activates change.

So, this first shift demands that we take responsibility for our perceptions, beliefs and experiences. Taking 100 percent responsibility is 100 percent empowering. It offers us choice and the ability to make change. We can't change others. We can only change ourselves; and when we do, everything begins to change for the better.

Let's take a closer look at what it means to take full responsibility and adopt empowering beliefs.

Taking Full Responsibility

1. Cause and effect

Cause and effect is a universal and natural law that states that everything that happens has a cause. We can also look at cause and effect from a perspective of empowerment. Cause and effect are two very different realities in which we can find ourselves. Where you find yourself is a matter of consciousness.

Those 'at effect' feel affected by people and circumstances and often end up making excuses and blaming others for the situations they find themselves in. These excuses could sound anything like this:

- I would be successful if it weren't for . . .
- It's not my fault.
- Things always go wrong for me.
- Why does it always happen to me?
- I'm being punished.
- I'm unlucky.

Such perceptions can seem very real but are not very useful. They effectively leave you feeling powerless to do anything about your situation.

The single most empowering mental shift we can make is a shift in consciousness from *effect* to *cause*.

Being 'at cause' is empowering. It means taking full responsibility, adopting an approach that says to the world:

- I am able to respond.
- I am in the driver's seat of my own life.
- I create my own reality.
- I accept that I am where I am because of decisions I made, either consciously or unconsciously. If I like where I am that's good. If I don't, I know I can change it.
- I have choices.
- I am in control of my mind and my thoughts and therefore my outcomes and results.

2. Results versus reasons

When we are 'at cause' we are in charge of the results. When 'at effect', we tend to come up with reasons and excuses for not achieving the results we wanted. Being 'at cause' means doing away with the reasons and excuses, and when you do, you begin to experience results.

3. Responsibility for results

It bears repeating: taking 100 percent responsibility for everything in your life is 100 percent empowerment. 'For everything?' you may ask. Yes, for everything that is happening in your universe.

This doesn't mean you need to blame yourself. No, it means taking charge of your thoughts and experiences, and being prepared to do some introspection: 'If the external world is a reflection of my internal world, what do I need to work on in myself or adjust in my own approach to make my world a better place?' When you take charge of your mind, thoughts and perceptions, you create your desired results every time.

4. Beliefs are self-fulfilling prophecies

This is the law of attraction. We don't believe things because they are true – beliefs become our truths because we believe them! We can achieve only what we believe we can. Any limitation is self-imposed. We can challenge our limiting beliefs because the truth is that we have infinite potential and ability.

Your nervous system is designed to give you what you focus on. For some reason we more often focus on what we don't want. How often do we say or think, 'I don't want to be ill' or 'I don't want to be late' or 'I don't want to fail'? These thoughts put us in a state of fear and anxiety.

So, you know what you don't want, but do you know what you do want? State your desires in the positive and in the present tense. For example, 'My timing is perfect', 'I can do this', 'I am naturally healthy'. Such thoughts put your mind – which creates your outcomes – in a positive and empowered state. Focus energizes and expands the probability of your thought. Focus on what you want, not on what you don't want.

> *'If you believe you can*
> *or if you believe you can't... you're right'.*
> **- HENRY FORD**

5. Our view of reality is a perception

We perceive the world through the filters of our own attitudes, values and beliefs. Therefore, we perceive the world not as it is but as we are. We create our own reality through our subjective perceptions. Then we project these perceptions out into the world and onto others.

Everything that we perceive outside of us is a projection from inside of us. Carl Jung said that our unconscious issues can be too deep-seated for us to uncover. We still have to learn from them, and in order to do so, we project them onto people around us. We then think these people are the problem, because we couldn't see the problems in ourselves. And so the learning begins.

We see ourselves in others, like a reflection in a mirror. What you see in others (what you like and don't like) is who you are yourself. Taking responsibility for our perceptions takes personal empowerment and transformation to a whole new level. When we take charge of our perceptions, we can change them any time. They're just perceptions, not truths! It's good practice to regularly question the way we perceive people and situations. When we change our perceptions, everything and everyone around us changes. And it happens quite magically. Life responds to us.

> *'Life does not just happen to you;*
> *you receive everything in your life based*
> *on what you've given'.*
> **- RHONDA BYRNE**

This first shift is a conscious decision; a deliberate mental shift from *effect* to *cause*; from *victim* to *creator*. After the initial decision, we may have to keep ourselves in check. When you find yourself in a challenging situation, watch your thoughts and reaction. Ask yourself: 'Am I now at *effect* or am I at *cause*? If I were at *cause*, how would I react differently?'

The mind is infinite in its creative ability:

- What you focus on determines your results
- What you believe to be real is real – for you
- What you focus on you energize and expand
- Focused energy transforms nothing into something
- When you change your beliefs and your perceptions, you change your reality – overnight!
- The inner creates the outer.

A note on karma

Cause and effect is also the cosmic law of karma, so it's worth getting this in perspective. 'Karma is a lack or absence of balanced experience' (Schwartz, 2012). Cause and effect is about learning; it's not a punishment. Karma simply translates as action. For every action there is a reaction; an effect. We all cultivate a karmic state or a karmic disposition, which is the result of our beliefs, values, intentions, thoughts and actions. This of course can change, and does change as we learn. Learning brings the unconscious programmes into conscious awareness, allowing us to make adjustments in our choices. When the learning is done, karma is done. We are then free to create a new reality.

Living Mindfully

By living mindfully, you align mind and body in the present moment, creating wholeness. Mindfulness helps broaden your awareness of your state of consciousness.

What is mindfulness?

- The ability to be fully present and connected to your experience in any given moment, in a curious, noncritical way

- Paying attention to your experiences from moment to moment

- Doing less and noticing more – learning how to be in the present moment

- Compassion towards yourself; acceptance of what you feel and experience

- Becoming conscious of that which is unconscious

- A way of being in the world you live in

- Like the sun; it only has to shine its light to do its transformational and healing work

- A coming to your senses; being associated in the experience with all senses. When you are dissociated, you know of the flower or sunset but are not able to really touch it with awareness.

Mindfulness is simply being fully aware of what you are doing in any given moment, which in turn clears the mind. Mindfulness is often practised through breathing exercises aimed at focusing your attention in the moment. It can also be practised in the form of mindful walking and mindful eating – the idea is that you can take this practice into everyday activities, really being in the present moment and remaining acutely aware of your environment and your experience.

The attitudinal foundations of mindfulness practice, although challenging, can help us broaden our awareness and observe habitual mental patterns.

What are the attitudinal foundations?

- **Non-judgement** – not labelling anything as good or bad, exciting or boring, easy or difficult; remaining an impartial witness

- **Patience** – being with your experience, with this moment, not rushing to the next; patience is a form of wisdom; a butterfly can't be helped out of a chrysalis

- **A beginner's mind** – staying open to learning, our knowing gets in the way of new learning

- **Trust** – believing in your own feelings, intuition, uniqueness and healing

- **Non-striving** – not having a goal; no need to get somewhere; this is about non-doing; just *being* (with) yourself, seeing and accepting things as they are – in the moment

- **Acceptance** – not resisting; this doesn't mean resigning or being satisfied with less; just accepting what is right now as the starting point; this is a precondition for healing

- **Letting go** – non-attachment; not hanging onto pleasure or avoiding pain; not holding onto summer or dreading winter; just letting your experience be, as it is; noticing and letting go of attachment to specific outcomes; letting go like you do when you go to sleep at night.

- **Non-doing** – just being

- **Wakefulness** – being aware

- **Connectedness** – being aware of our intrinsic wholeness and interconnectedness; wholeness is healing.

> *'When the mind is left without anything to cling to, it becomes still.'*
> **– SRI RAMANA MAHARSHI**

We will explore mindfulness from different perspectives and for different uses further along this journey. On this first step we use mindfulness for reflection.

Through mindfulness you can reflect on:

- **Your perceptions.** Our reality is just a perception coloured by our beliefs, values, memories and experiences. We always perceive subjectively. Ask yourself, 'What am I not seeing?'

- **Your beliefs.** These are self-fulfilling prophesies. Our beliefs create our realities. 'Do I believe I can do it?'

- **Your thoughts.** Be mindful of your self-talk. As you think so you create. 'Are my thoughts helping me?'

- **Your mind-body link.** Mind and body is one interconnected whole. Pain and emotions are messages from your unconscious mind. Unresolved suppressed emotions can cause disease in the body. 'What is my mind and body telling me?'

- **Your responsibility.** Taking 100% responsibility is 100% empowering. 'Am I taking responsibility for everything happening in my life?'

- **Cause and effect.** You choose between acting and reacting. 'Am I "at cause" or am I "at effect"?'

You'll be glad to know that mindfulness is not about clearing the mind of all thoughts but focusing your attention on one thing – for example, the breath. When your mind wanders, which it will, notice the thoughts and then bring your mind back to the one thing. Over time this disciplines the unruly mind and it becomes more focused.

Mindfulness Meditation

Sit upright, relaxed, spine comfortably straight. Let your shoulders hang naturally.

Rest your hands gently on your lap. Set your feet apart with soles on the ground; grounded.

Close your eyes or rest your gaze on a still object or spot a few feet in front of you. Relax your eyelids.

Start by setting your intention for the meditation: to be with your own experience and bring awareness to thoughts, feelings, beliefs and perceptions.

Now, bring your attention to your breathing, observing the natural rhythm of your breath.

No need to change the breathing in any way; just observe it like a curious explorer.

Pay attention to the breath; be aware of it, feel the sensation of it, not thinking about it.

Allow the breath to take centre stage in your awareness, just experiencing it.

Notice the sensation of the cool air in the nostrils as you breathe in and the warmer sensation as you breathe out.

Notice the little somersault of a turning point between the in-breath and the out-breath in the tip of the nostril. Notice the gap between the in-breath and the out-breath.

There is no right or wrong way to breathe. Just do it your way, observing curiously.

Bring a quality of kindness to your awareness – compassion, patience with yourself and your own experience, moment by moment.

Use the breath like an anchor to reconnect to the here and the now.

Thoughts and feelings may come and go. Just notice them, not judging them. Observe them with curiosity and awareness.

What images or feelings arise with the thoughts? People or events may pop up in your mind. What are your perceptions attached to these people and/or events?

Anything that comes up, own it, give it attention, sit with it and learn from it.

By staying mindful of our thoughts and feelings we start to let go of our habitual reactions.

Paying attention to the nature of our thoughts and feelings is something we don't often do. By doing so, we unify the conscious and unconscious minds.

As you sit with it, does the feeling change, perhaps into another feeling?

Are the thoughts and perceptions attached to the feeling changing as well?

Acknowledge these feelings as messages. Learn from these messages with compassion in your heart, without judging or avoiding them.

Learn in an effortless, reflective way. Then let it go. Release any concern about opinions too; releasing brings joy.

When the darkness goes the light sets in. Rest in the light. This is enlightenment that brings clarity. Be open and receptive to positive thoughts and feelings rising. These may be relief, lightness, calm, peace, care, kindness, love, self-love, joy and healing.

Then guide the mind back to the present breath, allowing full attention back on your breathing and the physical sensations of the breath.

Just be with each breath, in this moment, nothing to achieve. Simply allow your experience to be what it is, not wanting it to be anything else.

As you bring your practice to a close, gently lift your eyelids and bring your awareness to the room.

Take this reflective, mindful practice into your everyday existence, regularly shining the light of awareness and transformation on your thoughts, beliefs and perceptions.

Adapted from sources: Hanson (2009), Kornfield (2002) and Heaversedge and Halliwell (2010).

Visit *http://liftingtheveilsofillusion.co.uk/meditations/* to download a free audio mindfulness meditation.

Importance of the breath

Breath is life. As long as we breathe we are alive!

Breath is energy. Through breathing we generate energy.

Breath is spirit. As we breathe in – *inspire* – we take *in spirit*.

Benefits of breathing

The simple practice of deep breathing is the most effective way to:

- Energize yourself
- Detoxify – 70 percent of toxins in the body are released through breathing
- Relax
- Slow your heart rate
- Raise the level of your energy's vibration and feel uplifted
- Clear the mind
- Align your mind, body and spirit
- Restore balance.

Journey through the Chakras: First Chakra Contemplation and Visualization

Chakra	First chakra: the root chakra, at the base of the spine
Function	Survival instincts, sense of belonging, groupthink, culture, nation, safety, security, health, grounding
Emotion	Fear
Colour	Red
Spiritual Law	All is one
Meditation	I have
Element	Earth
Crystal	Garnet, ruby, red jasper, bloodstone, obsidian, hematite, smoky quartz

The base, or root, chakra is about our sense of stability and security, about safety and physical survival. Here we feel the earth's energy. This chakra is connected to our legs and feet, through which we ground ourselves and feel safe in the body. Feel yourself grounded to Mother Earth, your solid foundation from which you draw good health for the body. Appreciate the earth and feel grateful for your body, without which you could not experience mind and spirit. Here at the root we can experience stress and fear that hold us back, but we can also experience the courage to take action. Stand your ground. You have the right to be here. The colour of the root chakra is bright holly-berry red. Send your breath down into this chakra and visualize filling it with vivid-red vital energy. Then visualize this chakra opening like a red rose and vital energy flowing through it.

A Mindfulness Experience
To work . . .

I greeted the day, t'was cool and cloudy – not a promise of sun from above

A noisome breeze played in the open street,

Patiently I stood

The tram still some way off

Finally with a screech it arrived

Doors klonked open, hurried footsteps in and out as passengers loaded and unloaded...

Ding-ding... and with a jerk we're off

Sigh – no seats, content to stand, supported by an indecently bright yellow pole

More stops and starts

Surrounded by people

Alone

My stop,

Excuses made – out the door

Deep breath of fresh air

I wait for the mad rush to depart

Headphones in, contemplative music soothing

Slow stroll along canal

See the ripples on the water

The yellow bog irises and water lilies

Protected by a bubble

I'm surrounded with the ebb and flow of humanity

Flotsam in the tide

Desperate to get from somewhere to somewhere else

STOP!

Take a moment

Breathe

Look, Feel . . .

Give thanks – the world is a magical place

Humbled I move along

Shame it's all unseen as you hurry by

BY CALVIN RISKOWITZ
CLOUD EVANGELIST

Step 2: Transcending Fear

Illusion 2	The world is a dangerous place
	Fear IS the illusion
Reality	Fear exists only in the mind
	Fear is contractive and limiting
	You are always safe
	Love is all there is
	When the fear goes, you can access love and positivity and open up to your true potential
Shift	Honour emotions as messages
	Learn, and let go of all fear
Healing Meditation	Heal and release negative emotions

Transcending Fear, Doubt and Other Negative Emotions

Having made the empowering mental shift to full responsibility, we inevitably start an essential healing process. When we stop the blame, we begin to accept that we are where we are because of our own doing. We then begin to bring about necessary change. As we change, our lives change. Patterns and habits change and we can start letting go of the emotions, beliefs and baggage of the past. As we heal and release the issues of the past, we can make peace with them and create a clean slate. Every new day can be a total new beginning.

The Significance of Emotions

Most of us have grown up in a society that values intellect over emotions. We rarely show our emotions, let alone express them. Many common expressions in our language don't encourage a healthy approach to emotions: 'big boys don't cry'; 'bite your tongue', 'don't speak in anger'; 'count to 10 before you speak'. Keeping these phrases in mind can lead us to suppress our emotions. Consequently, we don't even acknowledge these emotions to ourselves. Anger, sadness, fear, hurt and guilt – these emotions make us feel uncomfortable, so we tend to avoid or suppress them. However, feeling these emotions is a normal, natural aspect of being human, and it's best to acknowledge and express them. From a therapeutic perspective, emotions aren't a problem unless they are unresolved or suppressed. Feelings must be acknowledged. They must be felt. Otherwise, they will linger and grow stronger. Eventually, unhealed emotions affect our physical health.

As with pain in the body, our emotions are actually messages from the unconscious mind. If you're feeling anger, for example, it might mean that someone overstepped your boundaries and it's time to reassert those boundaries. Anxiety tells us that the mind is focused on a feared outcome and thus energizing the very thing we don't want. Sadness, hurt and depression are often a result of feelings that remained unexpressed and are now turned inward. The beauty of the body is that it takes care of itself. Only our thoughts and beliefs interfere with this process. Research shows a link between suppressed emotions and illnesses such as cancer. There is also a link between anger and high blood pressure, and between hostility or cynicism and heart disease. Generally, people who are optimistic, who intuitively know they have a choice, who have the ability to let go, who can flow with change, who can laugh at themselves and who have a basic trust in people are robust and healthy (Edwards, 2010, Hanson, 2009; Heaversedge and Halliwell, 2010).

Knowing and accepting the feelings is the seed of healing. Paying attention to the emotion helps us to see it clearly, and so wisdom comes through attending to the feelings. A major source of suffering is wanting things 'our way'. Everything happens for our own learning and growth. We can't always see this when we're in the situation. Soon you'll look back and see how you have grown through it. Clear water reflects more light. When the murky waters of the unconscious mind are clear, wisdom shines through (Hanson, 2009).

Why Release Past Emotions?

The mind-body link

Negative emotions cause stress hormones; if these emotions are not worked through, they are stored in the body. Unresolved, suppressed emotions can cause disease in the body. The body reads the mind all the time. Deepak Chopra (1989) says: 'Our immune system continuously eavesdrops on our internal dialogue' (our self-talk, thoughts, beliefs). Stress literally causes the DNA strands to contract, wind tight and shut down, limiting the potential we can tap into. Conversely positive emotions cause DNA to relax and unwind so growth can take place, creativity can be tapped and new possibilities can be realised (Edwards, 2010).

Emotions can reflect familial and habitual reactive patterns. As an example we may habitually panic when we are out of our comfort zone or react with anger when we feel criticised. Such patterns can be learnt behaviour passed on in the family. Releasing emotions of the past is uplifting, healing and transformational. Once negative emotions are healed and released, we can begin to experience positive emotions. The old makes way for the new.

Emotions produce vibrations, and this ladder of emotional levels brilliantly illustrates the vibration rates of the various levels of consciousness. I have adapted the concepts in the following table from two key resources: Edwards (2010) and Hawkins (1995).

Emotional Levels

Mode of Being	Energy Vibration	Emotion	State	Consciousness
Wave mode of energy, creativity, imagination, infinite potential	700-1000	Enlightenment		Connectedness Higher self At cause
	600	Bliss, peace		
	540	Joy		
	500	Unconditional love		
	400	Clarity, understanding		
	350	Forgiveness, acceptance	Transcendence	
	310	Hope, contentment, gratitude, optimism, positivity	Expanded consciousness, seeing the bigger picture	
	250	Trust, satisfaction		Starting to take some responsibility
	200	Courage, affirmation	Empowerment	
Particle Mode of form	175	Pride, self-righteousness		Starting to release some resistance
Stress: Fight	150	Anger, resentment, envy, jealousy, frustration, irritation, impatience, control, obsession		
	125	Desire, craving, enslavement, addiction, disappointment		

Flight	100	Fear, insecurity, feeling overwhelmed, worry, doubt		
Freeze	75	Grief, regret	Despondence	
	50	Pessimism, boredom, apathy, despair, depression, disempow-erment		
	30	Guilt, blame		
	20	Shame, feeling unworthy, self-sacrifice, feeling trapped or controlled	Victimhood	Separateness Ego At effect

Logarithmic calibrations of energy-vibratory
frequencies on a scale from 0–1000

Where You Dwell In Emotions, There You Dwell In Consciousness

It's natural to experience the whole range of emotions. One day you may feel optimistic and positive, and then comes a day when you feel low for no apparent reason. The questions you must keep asking yourself are: 'Where on this ladder of emotions do I find myself most of the time?' and 'What emotions do I need to release to climb the ladder of consciousness?' The emotions we feel on the bottom rungs of the ladder can make us feel stuck because the energy vibrates at such a low frequency here. On these rungs, we feel we are victims of circumstances, and over time this can affect our health. Fear- and anger-related emotions start to generate energy and movement as we decide to fight or flee. Developing a healthy ego may bring some relief. With self-interest still a major motivator, we may from time to time be pushing against the flow of life. When we release resistance and take responsibility, we begin to climb into positive emotions. We are not entirely free from the ego until we are truly able to practise acceptance and forgiveness. This is easier when we remember that we are one interconnected whole. With forgiveness, we finally transcend the ego and become more of who we truly are – our true higher selves. Clarity brings wisdom, and previously elusive emotions such as unconditional love, joy and peace are finally experienced as our true, natural state. Youthfulness and good health, also our natural state, returns.

Emotional levels – as measured on this energy frequency scale from 0 to 1000 – are levels of consciousness. Where you dwell in emotions, there you dwell in consciousness. Consciousness, not DNA, is your blueprint for health. Consciousness changes the DNA; new possibilities open up and good health returns (Edwards, 2010).

Transformational therapies facilitate gentle yet powerful processes that enable you to heal emotions of the past. Anger, sadness, fear, hurt and guilt keep us attached to the past, and as we heal these emotions, we set ourselves free – free to create a new, magnificent life. All healing is a release of fear. A powerful statement in meditation is: 'I release ...' (e.g., this fear, this anger).

I highly recommend transformational therapy sessions that facilitate a complete clearing-out of negative emotions and limiting beliefs. Equally effective is a healing meditation, described below, that I use during workshops for emotional healing. This meditation combines transformational techniques and a healing journey adapted from Deepak Chopra's *Syncrodestiny* (2003).

Emotions and memories are stored in clusters, or gestalts according to Carl Jung (James & Woodsmall, 1988). To heal past emotions, it is always good to find the root cause of the cluster and learn from it. This meditation facilitates that process wonderfully and can be repeated by yourself whenever you feel emotions rising.

Meditation: Healing Past Emotions

Find a place where you can peacefully and comfortably enter a meditative state. This meditation will guide you on an inner healing journey.

Imagine that your memory is like a film that you can rewind. Right now, rewind the film of your life to just yesterday. What were some of the things you did during the day? Did anything cause you fear, upset or anger? You may have felt impatient or frustrated when something did not happen quickly enough, or someone might have been abrupt or inconsiderate. For the next moment or so, recall the events of the day in as much detail as you can. Focus on a moment of fear, upset or anger, becoming aware of the sensations in your body as well as the emotions in your mind. What are you learning? Let the lesson come to you from your heart. You may see different perspectives, have new insights.

Then, rewind the film of your life back to approximately a year ago. What were you doing? What was on your mind at that time? Do you recall being afraid, upset or angry about something? Really feel the emotions of that time in your mind and in your body. Are the feelings the same as the feelings you remember feeling yesterday? What are you learning?

Rewind the film of your life back to when you were a teenager. Again, recall a situation that caused you fear, upset or anger as a teenager. Relive the feelings, mentally and physically. Notice how the emotion that you experienced yesterday has been built on emotions from so long ago. What are you learning?

Now bring to mind an incident from your childhood. What was the earliest time you experienced fear, upset or anger? Bring that experience into your awareness. Where were you when it happened? Who else was there? Who or what was it that caused you to feel this way? Feel all the sensations created by that emotion. What are you learning?

Notice how the fear, upset and anger have accumulated over the years. Although you may not remember it, there was a time in your life before you ever felt these things. How were you when you were fearless? How were you when your life was one exciting, curious adventure? A time of positivity, bliss and peace? Imagine what that experience of pure joy might have been like.

Focus on a time before any fear, upset or anger. Rewind that imaginary film of your life until the screen goes white, and feel the boundaries between yourself and your surroundings evaporate. For the next minute or so, experience the loss of your ego, and all your accumulated fear, upset and anger.

With that feeling of pure bliss still in your awareness, begin to move that imaginary film of your life forward again. Visit the same points in your life at which you stopped earlier – those angry, upsetting or fearful moments from your childhood, your teenage years, a year ago and yesterday. As you relive these scenes, flood them with the experience of bliss. Instead of allowing one moment of anger or fear to build upon another, release these emotions one by one, from earliest childhood to just yesterday. Spend a moment or so feeling this bliss replace the old emotions. Allow the toxic build-up of years of fear, upset and anger to be released from your mind, body and soul.

You can repeat this healing meditation any time to address emotions at their roots. Many people find it especially useful at night, just before they go to sleep. They wake up peaceful and without any residual emotions.

Emotions can also be released very effectively the mindful way. Visit _http://liftingtheveilsofillusion.co.uk/meditations/_ to download a free audio meditation: Healing Emotions the Mindful Way.

Living a Life Free from Fear

Can you live a life free from fear? Is it possible? What is the root cause of fear? According to Buddha, maintaining the illusions of the three-dimensional world (the tangible, material world of particles) creates all our suffering. The ego's investment in a specific outcome creates all our suffering and fear.

And according to cell biologist Bruce Lipton (2005), 95 percent of all modern-day ill-health is caused by stress. Genetic conditions, such as Down's syndrome, comprise the other 5 percent. We think our busy lives cause stress. In reality, our thinking causes stress – our fear-based thoughts. 'What ifs' about all manner of things that could go wrong are projected ahead of us into the future. These thoughts are always about what we don't want to happen. When we do this habitually, the fear causes stress which in turn causes physical discomfort and disease. Our bodies are not designed to be in prolonged fearful, stressful states. Is it becoming apparent that approaching health at only the physical level is quite limiting? Indeed, the body is simply an expression of the mind – the law of cause and effect at play.

Thankfully we live in a time when a shift from this fear-based worldview is not only possible but commonplace. What is the alternative? What are we shifting into?

Our nervous systems have a sympathetic division and parasympathetic division. The sympathetic division controls the fight or flight (stress) response, and the parasympathetic the relaxed and creative response.

In modern-day life with its fast pace and pressures, we spend more time in the sympathetic nervous system than is good for us. Consequently, feeling stressed out, the body goes on orange or red alert, emotions intensify and we are set up for fear and frustration. When we are in this mode too long and too often, our quality of life is soon affected, as well as our mental and physical health. Many of us don't often experience the extremes but live a life on simmer, experiencing an ongoing low-grade form of stress that we hardly detect consciously (Hanson, 2009). We often blame the pressures of life and our workload for feeling stressed out, but stress is not a result of the external conditions themselves but the way we think about them. External stresses may even be good for us, stretching us and helping us to learn and grow. Internal stress, caused by our own perceptions, beliefs, thoughts and feelings regarding the external events – this is the real cause of negative stress. But this is good news because it means we can do something about our stress levels. By watching these thoughts and feelings and becoming aware of any unnecessary underlying simmering, we can intentionally shift out of the stress nervous system into the relaxed and creative nervous system.

So, how do we shift into this nervous system? By adopting its qualities.

The following chart illustrates this shift in approach:

The Nervous System

Sympathetic nervous system Stress: Fight, flight and freeze	Parasympathetic nervous system Relaxation and creativity
Negative emotions: fear, anger, etc.	Positive emotions: joy, peace, etc.
Past/future	NOW
Limiting beliefs/doubts	Creativity, imagination, infinite potential
Disease	Health and youthfulness

Focus/tunnel vision	Expanded awareness
Ego/head/thought	True self/heart/feeling
Serious	Lighthearted, fun
Lonely and separate	Connected, all is one
Constricted	Expansive
DNA wound up; tight	DNA unwound; unlimited potential
Small and limited	Magical, infinite, unbound
Duality: rights and wrongs	Unity – beyond duality Just is – an experience
Struggle upstream	Flow with life effortlessly

Effect:
  Life happens to me
  I am a victim of circumstances
  Life is unfair
	Cause:
	  I create my own reality
	  I feel empowered and take charge
	  Life is an adventure

Rapid, shallow breathing	Deep, slow breathing
Three-dimensional world of form	Energy world of potentiality

The more you deliberately shift into the relaxed, creative mode of being, the more you reclaim your potential.

A miracle is a shift in perception from fear to love, Marianne Williamson reminds us in her reflections on the Course in Miracles (Williams,1992)

- Practise being present, intentionally guiding the thoughts out of the past, out of the future and back into the moment of now.

- Make time for fun and laughter. Seriousness is the first sign of stress.

- Intentionally bring activity into your day that will boost positive emotions such as calm, peace and joy. Get fresh air. Stare at a bee on a flower. Observe the natural curiosity and contagious joy of a child.

- Incorporate gratitude into your daily life – this is one of the quickest ways of shifting into the relaxed nervous system. Perhaps make this part of your meditative practice; reflect on all the good things in your life. Count your blessings. Gratitude not only changes your mood instantly, it is also a powerful magnet that attracts more good things into your life.

- Change your breathing. Diaphragmatic breathing – deep in-breath and long out-breath – is a great practice to combine with meditation. This form of breathing is both energizing and calming. When you've become familiar with this practice, a single breath, like a sigh, can take you into restorative relaxation.

- Engage in creative activities – the kind that seem to make time stand still. They will benefit you greatly, and when aligned with your purpose, they can be very meaningful. Also, be creative just for the fun of it. It opens you up to the magic of this world.

- Practise self-hypnosis aimed at expanding your field of awareness by activating peripheral vision (see illustration below: Peripheral vision), a technique described about 160 years ago by James Braid, the inventor of hypnosis (James, 2000).

Meditation: Expanded Awareness by Activating Peripheral Vision

This is an exercise in self-hypnosis, relaxation and expanded awareness. Peripheral vision engages the parasympathetic nervous system. It puts us in a relaxed, creative and resourceful state. This state is a great place to learn, as here the unconscious mind is wide open and soaks up everything. It's a state of heightened awareness; a state in which no negative thought can be held.

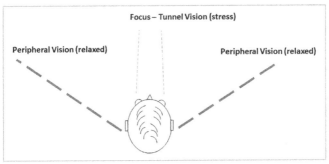

'Peripheral vision'

Expanded awareness by activating peripheral vision

We can only be imaginative and creative when we are relaxed:

- Pick a spot on the wall in front of you, slightly above eye level

- With the eyes fixed on that spot, pay attention to the peripheral part of your vision

- Soften your gaze and expand your awareness into the periphery

- Relax the jaw

- You'll enter a daydreaming state, a trance state – this is often how we drive, and it's safe; you may miss your turn-off, but you'll see everything around you

- Think of an issue causing you stress – you may have to go back to the one spot on the wall to hold a negative thought

- Expand your awareness into your peripheral vision again. Notice how you can eventually take the whole room into your peripheral vision

- Notice how the problem disappears as you enter this relaxed state of expanded awareness

- Now do the same with your eyes closed

- Bring your attention to your breathing

- Deepen the in-breath and make the out-breath twice as long

- Find a spot of light or colour or an imagined spot in the centre of your inner vision, slightly above the eyes

- Now in much the same way as you did with the spot on the wall, focus on this spot of light and expand your awareness into the peripheral part of your inner vision

- Allow your awareness to expand wider and wider, into the nothingness

- Enter the void at the far left and the far right of your inner peripheral vision

- If there is any remnant of an issue, take it into the void with you – it came from the void, everything is created from the void, and now you can uncreate any unwanted thought by taking it back to the void – watch it disappear into the void

- You can also tap into the void to create resourceful states; e.g., inner strength, clarity, calm and confidence.

Visit *http://liftingtheveilsofillusion.co.uk/meditations/* to download a free audio meditation: Peripheral Vision, an exercise in self-hypnosis.

You may wonder if you can go through life in the parasympathetic nervous system. People often ask me this. Surely, they say, I can't go through life in a relaxed state all the time, can I? Don't I need a bit of a buzz and energy to do things? Well, consider a pet cat.

It may serve as a good example of your natural state of being. For most of the day it is likely in a relaxed, playful state. It may shift into the sympathetic nervous system for about 10 minutes to catch a mouse, or to fight off another cat, only to return to rest mode again. We seem to go the other way around, taking about 10 minutes out of a busy day to relax. Our modern-day lives have clearly shifted quite out of balance. In the book *Buddha's Brain* (2009), Rick Hanson explains that ultimately we aim to keep the nervous system as a whole in balance. This balance can be achieved when we make the parasympathetic nervous system our baseline. From this baseline the sympathetic nervous system can be activated for enthusiasm, vitality, drive and passion. Occasional spikes in the sympathetic nervous system help us deal with a demanding boss at work or a challenging teenager at home. Ideally, we take our relaxed, creative state into these demanding situations. This will afford us a broader perspective as we bring our creative mind, intuition and inner wisdom to the issue at hand.

Ditch the Fear for Good

Can you make this shift and ditch the stress and fear for good? This is my greatest desire for you. Where we find ourselves in life is a matter of perceptions. The mind can be retrained to adopt and live by the qualities of the parasympathetic nervous system. When you relax, the mind can open up and you can be infinitely creative. Healing and releasing stress, negative emotions and limiting beliefs enables you to access your true magical self and live your life creatively, purposefully and joyfully.

'All healing is essentially a release of fear'.
- A COURSE IN MIRACLES

'And as we let our own light shine, we unconsciously
give other people permission to do the same.
As we are liberated from our own fear, our
presence automatically liberates others.
- MARIANNE WILLIAMSON, 1992.

As we release our fear, we lift the energy vibration level of the whole, and we heal the planet.

Journey through the Chakras: Second Chakra Contemplation and Visualization

Chakra	Second chakra: the sacral chakra, below the navel
Function	Sexuality, emotions, moving forward, material abundance, connection, pleasure, procreation, appetite, life purpose, creativity
Emotion	Fear, guilt, sadness
Colour	Orange
Spiritual Law	Honour one another
Meditation	I feel
Element	Water
Crystal	Carnelian, amber, orange calcite

Named after the sacrum, the sacral chakra is a sacred place; the centre of sexuality, pleasure, desire, procreation, creativity and financial abundance; the life force. The element is water, the centre of our emotions. Emotions are movement of energy. Healthy emotions have the same fluidity as water. Where in the root chakra we ground ourselves, here we centre ourselves, so we find balance between giving and receiving, others and self. Being centred brings us a sense of harmony. Where in the first chakra we focus on survival, here we start sharing what we have with others. Honour your emotions and let them flow. Release any guilt and fear. When fear goes you can open up to your creative energy. It is also important to distinguish between our own and others' emotions and guard against taking on others' emotions. This centre's colour is orange – the orange of a setting sun or of amber. Visualize this chakra opening and a warming orange glow flowing through it.

WE ARE NOT OUR FEAR!

Fear came knocking at my door!

I let him in
I don't know why!
He sat by my fire
Sipping hot tea,
Warm and comfortable in compatible company!
And I let him in.
I don't know why!

He spun wild imaginary tales
with
Visionary reality.
Tales that made my stomach churn.
A monstrous apparition;
From projected reflection.
And I let him in!
I listened to his words.
Fighting the pain in my brain of distorted delusion,
Tortured and stunned by the noise and confusion.
He didn't want to leave.
Who can blame him!
Fed and nurtured like a precious child
Nestled in the comfort of my misplaced trust!
But now!
Now
it's time to let him go
To disempower this monstrous illusion,

Through its release
For love and wisdom are knocking at my door!!!

If 'fear' returns I'll show him love
And perhaps I'll offer a cup of tea
'Cos now I've seen through all his tricks
I'll not let fear make a puppet of me

by Lynne Whalley,
Great Harwood

Step 3: Becoming a Magical Creator of Your Life

Illusion 3	Only what I can see and touch is real
	I have only this conscious mind
Reality	You are a multidimensional being moving between dimensions to create your reality
	You have three minds and four bodies
Shift	Open up to the unseen magical realm
	Become a magical creator of your life
Manifestation Meditation	Create, communicate
	Set intention, ask

There's More to Life than Meets the Eye

You are a multidimensional being moving between dimensions to create your reality.

You have three minds and four bodies (more on this in Step 5). A small part of you lives in this tangible world of particles that you can see and touch. The essence of who you are lives in the unseen, magical realms. These outlandish dimensions operate on a complete different set of rules – beyond time and space. They are truly magical, and so are you; a powerful wizard.

LIFTING THE VEILS OF ILLUSION

> ## What is magic?
>
> - The ability to recognize and understand the underlying forces of nature and the laws that govern them
> - A divine act that benefits humankind
> - Change created through subtle, unseen causes
> - Change created in the external environment by making wilful change in yourself
>
> All magic is mind magic, and it always involves transformation.

The Dimensions in which You Exist

The three-dimensional earth plane

This is the tangible world of particles and form that you can see and touch and experience with your physical body and are aware of with your conscious mind during your everyday waking state. Here you experience yourself as a separate individual in the solid world run on reliable and predictable scientific principles. Your ego mind – your conscious mind – has many vested interests here, where it reigns in its limited domain.

The fourth dimension

This is the astral plane that you frequent while sleeping and dreaming. It is the plane of your magical unconscious mind, your creative emotional mind. Because it is quantum physical in nature (more on this below), thoughts, emotions and feelings manifests much more quickly into reality here. Your unconscious mind brings about desired outcomes magically – by taking a quantum leap. Anything you can imagine is possible. As you imagine it you create it.

The fifth dimension

A heavenly place, this is the plane of your higher self – your eternal, divine, creative self. It is a place of pure potentiality: the quantum physicist's field of pure energy. It is a place of perfection, where thought manifest instantly. This dimension is beyond time and space, where there is only NOW – the first dimension beyond duality. All is one, interconnected whole. Pure light. Pure heart-based consciousness. The idea of fifth-dimensional living is expanded on in Step 7.

How Your Minds Work Together in the Creation Process

Your conscious mind (logical mind):

- Processes information
- Analyses
- Decides what you want
- Sets goals and intentions
- Gets specific about what you want
- Focuses on what you want
- Operates in linear time
- Visualizes what you want and thereby serves as an instruction to your unconscious mind.

Your unconscious mind (creative mind):

- Comprises your imagination, feelings, emotions
- Runs your body, your energy and your health
- Stores your memories and beliefs
- Operates on your instructions, your thoughts, your intentions
- Achieves your goals for you

- Works magic in the *how* of achieving your goal
- Takes a quantum leap (in time and process).

Your higher consciousness (higher self):

- Is your guiding spirit
- Is the creator in you
- Gives you what you ask for – always
- Is beyond time and space
- Has the blueprint for perfect health
- Doesn't fix or heal; instead creates another reality of perfection (more on this in Step 7).

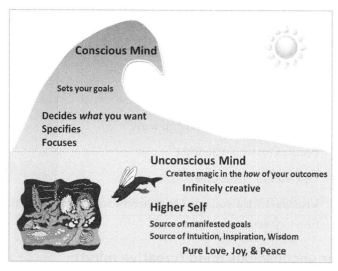

'How your minds work together in the creation process'

It's Your Imagination

Visualization and imagination are powerful creation tools. The words *imagining, imagination, imaging, image* and *magic* all have the same root.

To visualize is to create an image. Your conscious mind starts the creation process. By visualizing something, you present your unconscious mind, your magical mind, with an exact image of what you want. With your imagination, you excite and motivate your unconscious mind and set the creation process in motion. Magic begins!

Everything is created first as a thought; an idea. When you want to build a new house, first you create it in your mind. You may then discuss your ideas with an architect, who will draw up a plan that specifies all the exact details. Drawing something or writing it down with as many details as possible takes it from mere idea to reality. The builder takes the plan and starts putting one brick on top of another until you have your house. Everything is created like that: thought, then word, then deed.

Just Ask!

The image above outlines the process in which your three minds work together to manifest what you want. Your conscious mind decides what you want and directs your unconscious mind, your creative mind. Your unconscious mind in turn takes the request to your higher self, the creator in you. There is no direct link between your conscious mind and your higher self. You cannot consciously conceive of your higher self. Herein lies a secret to manifestation: your unconscious mind, your emotional, intuitive, creative, imaginative mind is the pathway to your higher self.

We approach the higher self when we want to achieve goals, create our desired future and heal ourselves and others. The means of manifestation are intention, goal-setting, seed meditation (taking an intention into a meditation), visualization and prayer.

For your minds to work together effectively and magically manifest what you want, your unconscious mind needs to be free from negative emotions and limiting beliefs. It needs to feel deserving of the abundance of the universe (Freedom Long, 1953).

Your higher self always gives you what you ask for. Therefore be careful what you ask for. You may well get it. Your higher self respects free will and must be asked. This is not asking like a helpless child: 'Please help me' or 'please give me'. Asking means aligning yourself with the creator in you and becoming a creator. It means invoking the divine creative power (more on this in Step 7).

Quantum Model of the Universe

To understand how your unconscious mind creates magic in the subtle world of energy, it helps to have an understanding of the quantum universe.

The law of causality – cause and effect – says that A causes B which results in C. Carl Jung observed connections between events without one being the cause of the other. This is what he called synchronicity, and he suggested that coincidences worked in this way. Synchronicity is the simultaneous occurrence of two meaningful events with no apparent causal connection (Snowden, 2006). Modern quantum physics allows for acausal effects in its physical theories. Synchronicity can be observed everywhere in nature – birds flying in formation and a school of fish moving as one. These creatures seem to communicate miraculously. Scientists wanted to learn about this seemingly instant communication, and they found that it comes through a connection shared in a unifying field.

Just like nature, we too interact with this unseen field all the time. We are multidimensional beings, living in more than one world – this one and the subtle worlds behind the veils. This field is where we go to start the creation process through imagination. To enter the field, we must be relaxed and activate our creative, imaginative mind.

In a quantum universe, energy and consciousness are inseparable (Chopra, 2003). Conscious focus creates the energy to change nothing into something. Consciousness determines whether light acts as a wave or a particle (Talbot, 1991).

Quantum Physics

World of Form and Particles	Energy World of Waves of Potentiality
Objects are real and solid	Everything is energy
The universe is objective	Your universe is subjective
Everything can be proven scientifically	The universe is holographic
Reality is a given	Reality is a construct of the mind. You create your reality with your thoughts
Separateness	Interconnectedness; oneness
The past creates the present and the future	Everything is created in the NOW
People are just human beings	People are unlimited creators
I have to know everything!	Confusion precedes a higher level of understanding
Stress, fear, limitation, scarcity	Infinity, abundance and pure potential
Effect	Cause

How We Create Reality in a Quantum Universe

- Everything is energy
- Energy follows thought
- As you think so you create
- Your universe is a subjective hologram
- Reality is a construct of the mind

- Everything starts with a thought; an idea that we energize through focus
- Focused energy transforms nothing into something
- Your nervous system is designed to give you what you focus on
- You create your reality with your thoughts
- Everything is one interconnected whole.

The Manifestation Process

The manifestation process in the three-dimensional world of form – the world of your conscious mind:

- action, effort, hard work, struggle, wading through treacle, slow and frustrating

The manifestation process in the fourth-dimensional world of emotions – the world of your unconscious mind:

- feeling good, believing you can, using positive affirmations, visualization and vision boards – as described by Rhonda Byrne in *The Secret* (2006)

The manifestation process in the fifth-dimensional world of thought – the world of your higher self:

- Thoughts create outcomes – at this level of refined vibrations, thoughts manifest into form much more quickly

- Take your awareness and consciousness into the heart

- Manifest from the heart, in the moment of now – the heart-brain is more powerful than the head-brain and has a vastly expanded electromagnetic field (Edwards, 2010 and *https://www.heartmath.org/articles-of-the-heart/science-of-the-heart/the-energetic-heart-is-unfolding/*)

- When you truly operate from the heart as your higher self you already have everything you need

- All longing and needs are gone: 'I have everything', 'I don't need all that'

- All lack or inadequacies are gone: 'My life is perfect', 'Everything and everyone is perfect'.

5-dim   4-dim   3-dim
Spirit → Thought → Emotions → Action/Effort → Manifestation
The dimensional manifestation process

Creating Your Own Reality

Do you believe you can do it? To be the powerful creator that you are, always challenge any self-limiting belief. These beliefs are not always easy to detect as they often exist at an unconscious level. Beliefs develop as we grow up and can embed themselves in the unconscious mind at a young age. They originate based on the people and institutions we grew up with and are essentially tribal beliefs.

In their 'Manifesting What You Really Want' seminar, Drs Wayne Dyer and Deepak Chopra speak about the importance of leaving behind our tribal consciousness. They point out that tribal consciousness holds us back by passing on belief systems based on scarcity, lack and helplessness. For example, Deepak Chopra says that no illness is ever due to a pathogen and that it is a misleading idea in medicine. Fascinating coming from a medic himself.

Thus, we have to do a bit of soul searching to bring these beliefs into our conscious awareness and challenge them. They are easy to challenge because they are based on an illusion; a false belief of who you are and what you are capable of doing. Exposing the false beliefs sets you free to adopt the kinds of beliefs you want to live by; empowering beliefs that enable you to magically create your desired outcomes.

Becoming the creator of your own reality means breaking from tribal beliefs. Carl Jung called this a process of individuating (Snowden, 2006). Essentially, this means developing a healthy ego that affords us assertiveness and confidence. Only by fulfilling the ego are we able to eventually move beyond it.

To uncover these tribal beliefs, we may have to question and challenge every societal belief. Until we question them, we take them as givens, as truths.

Tribal Beliefs

- Beliefs about abilities; e.g., I can do this and can't do this; this is possible and this is not
- Beliefs about intelligence; e.g., IQ tests and exam results determine the clever and the not-so-clever
- Beliefs about health; e.g., certain conditions run in the family, it's genetic
- Beliefs about God; e.g., God is judgemental and punishes sins
- Beliefs about age; e.g., people retire when they are 60
- Beliefs about social roles and expectations; e.g., it's right to put other people first
- Beliefs about men; e.g., men are insensitive
- Beliefs about women; e.g., woman are emotional
- Beliefs about rights and wrongs; e.g., it's right to… and it's wrong to…

Manifestation Belief Gremlins

- It's only a dream
- Will it ever happen?
- I don't think it will work
- I can't do it
- I'm not good enough
- What if I fail?
- What if I'm successful?
- What will people think?
- I don't deserve it
- I need to work hard at it
- I can't afford it
- I don't have the confidence
- Money is the root of all evil
- People can't be trusted
- Hang onto your job, times are tough
- Your pension is your security
- There isn't enough

Such beliefs can be very subtle and can run undetected in the background like programmes until we challenge them and expose them for what they are: simply limiting beliefs. Remember, we don't believe things because they are true. Rather, things become true because we believe them. This is all too evident in the placebo effect that doctors often witness when they prescribe tablets that are nothing but sugar and their patients heal themselves.

Voice Management

Becoming a powerful co-creator of your life is all about managing the voices in your head.

LIZARD VOICE	WIZARD VOICE
It's a struggle	It can be done effortlessly
It's difficult	It's easy
I'm trying	I'm going for it!
I have a duty, an obligation	I am free
I should, have to, shouldn't, couldn't	I can, I want to
I feel fear	I feel love and joy
I'm not good enough	I have infinite potential
I don't deserve it	I can be and do and have anything I want
What if I fail?	There is no failure, only experience
Life is against me	Life is a magical adventure
What if things go wrong?	Just imagine how great it would be
I can't do it	I am infinitely creative and imaginative
I don't know how to	My mind is magical and can bring it about
I have no choice	I can choose between infinite possibilities
I'm stuck	I am always growing and evolving
I don't care	I have empathy and compassion
I am nothing; I don't have enough	I am a much-loved child of an abundant universe
I am just a human being	I am unique, valuable and divinely inspired
I must be in control	I can adapt and go with the flow in faith and trust that all will work out well

The future is uncertain	I can enjoy each moment as my life unfolds perfectly
I am constricted, stressed	I have everything it takes to succeed; expanded, I can do anything I put my mind to

Trust your inner wizard. Faith and trust transcend the ego's lizard voice. Change *should* and *need* into *can* and *want to*. Do what you do from a place of love, joy, freedom, growth, expansion, creativity, imagination and inspiration.

Shifting from fear to love means evolving into the higher being that you are. All consciousness is connected; therefore, when you shift fear and release limiting tribal beliefs, you help the tribe to evolve.

'If the sun and moon should doubt,
they would immediately go out'.
- WILLIAM BLAKE

As a magical creator you want to be truly free from tribal expectations, walk your own path, live your own purpose and create your own reality.

The following healing meditation facilitates the process of cutting yourself away from tribal consciousness. Follow this with intent to raise your own consciousness out of the collective so you can stand in your own right, power and purpose.

Healing Meditation: Cutting from Tribal Connections

- Breathe
- Empty the mind of thoughts
- Close your eyes
- Relax body top to toes
- Let the world fade away
- Go inside.

See yourself standing in a wide road. Ahead of you is a magnificent spiritual mountain. Notice what is holding you back: guilt, fear, anger, blame, doubt. Collective fears and limiting beliefs can hold us back, and the biggest is the fear of financial lack – not trusting the universe will support you. The media often fuels these fears. This is the tribal consciousness you are going to cut yourself from now, for good. You can truly be outside collective fear. And as you cut yourself from these fears and limiting beliefs, do so with love and appreciation for those who raised you. For each of us there comes a time to separate from past beliefs and become our own person. All you do is cut away from the illusion and step into your own truth.

So, if there are any niggly fears or doubts, any issues of the past, negative memories of the past, place them on the road behind you. Identify any future concerns, any causes for worry and anxiety. Place these on the road in front of you. These limiting beliefs can sometimes be visualized or even felt as stains in our energy field or sticky strands binding us into the collective unconscious.

Now begin to cut those strands. Visualize yourself cutting them away, as you would with spider web strands. Keep cutting, clearing them all away.

After a while, see the mist rolling in, covering the road behind and in front of you. See yourself standing in the mist, cocooned in the mist. It's a soothing, cleansing, purifying mist. Something about the energy in this mist clears and cleanses you, sets you free. It clears the stains and dissolves all remaining strands.

And now the mist lifts and you feel very different. You find yourself standing on a mountaintop from where you can see everything clearly. You are your own person, free from past conditioning, limiting beliefs and fears. Free from opinions, free to follow your dreams, free to be true to yourself, regardless of others' ideas. You can see all around you, clearly – wide and far. You can see everything just the way you want it now. See yourself in good shape, embracing a new sense of power and inner strength, on top of things. The sun is shining down on you. A golden sun drenches this mountaintop. You stand in these rays of light, bright rays of light shining down on you, and a very special feeling comes over you.

Really feel you are stepping into your own; your own purpose. Some people describe it as a glow – that point in your life when things seem to be going right for you and you really feel great. Just allow that special feeling to come over your body, a feeling of deep faith and trust in the universe and in yourself. As you experience this feeling, recognize the degree to which your unconscious mind will allow you to maintain a sense of power, purpose, inner strength, trust and confidence.

Each breath of air that you take into your body on this mountaintop makes you feel expanded, strong and powerful. Your mind is all-powerful and you now use it to visualize a positive outcome for you, just the way you want it. The old fear and doubt is gone now, making way for your creative energy to return. Feel yourself filled with this positive, creative mental energy. You have this sense of being the creator of your life. You're filled with a new sense of purpose, meaning and happiness – there is so much to enjoy and look forward to.

Time stands still for you on this mountaintop as you enjoy this higher vision. Many others are walking up the sun-drenched path to the mountaintop: others like you, and many light beings are there to assist you. Feel yourself expand as you take in everything, all the vastness. You know that not only do you have access to the resources and abundance of that vastness, but you are also part of that vastness and totally supported by the entire universe. Feel that power and safety and greatness inside and all around you now.

You can see so much, and on this hill, you feel a new surge of confidence, power and belief in your ability to create your life just as you want it, magically.

As you stand in this light, imagine how your life will be now that you are living it as the powerful creator that you are. On this mountaintop you step into this power as you put past doubt aside for good. And now you know, remember, how to use the power of positive thoughts. The results you achieve in your life have everything to do with what the voice in your head tells you. What are you saying to yourself now? How do you feel about yourself now? Notice how you stand taller. What are the new messages you want to send to yourself and others?

And now you know you really can do anything you put your mind to. Welcome change, enjoy taking risks – because anything is possible, you know.

You feel excited about what you can be and do and have, and you are free to choose and that is so empowering.

Just allow these images and feelings to help you. Take all these good images and feelings with you from the mountaintop; pause briefly to give thanks to the light beings, knowing they are always there for you. As you begin to walk across a beautiful colourful meadow along a lovely path, you feel free. And now you reach the edge of the field, knowing how you have changed in many ways. You stand in your wide road again – is it the same road or are you walking a different road now? Either way, you can see the horizon clearly, and you are filled with anticipation of all those good things coming to you. Begin re-orienting yourself to this time, this place and become aware of feeling refreshed, alert, comfortable, and with a deep sense of having accomplished something of great importance just for you.

- Become aware of your body again
- Stretch
- Take a deep breath and energize yourself
- Ground back into the body.

Visit *http://liftingtheveilsofillusion.co.uk/meditations/* to download a free audio meditation: Cutting from tribal connections.

My New Empowering Belief

Now you are free to adopt your own empowering beliefs. Write them down and reinforce them in your mind until they become anchored within it.

Formulate your own new empowering beliefs to live by and remind yourself of them often, until they are second nature. For example:

I am a powerful and magical co-creator of my life.

I have a divine ability to attract and manifest all that I desire in life.

I trust in the divine wisdom that's in me.

I deserve to experience the abundance of the universe.

The infinite universal creative force is in me.

With the power of my mind I create all my desired outcomes.

We Need High-vibration Energy to Create and Manifest

One of the most effective ways to energize yourself is through breathing. Diaphragmatic breathing is particularly effective because it generates energy while reducing anxiety, raising you to finer levels of vibration. The diaphragm is the muscle beneath the lungs that helps you breathe. Place your hand on the stomach below the ribcage to ensure the stomach and not just the chest rises and falls with the breath (Hanson, 2009). Breathe with a 1-to-2 ratio (deep in-breath, out-breath twice as long) – this is both energizing and calming. Do this for 10 to 20 minutes to generate energy, align your three minds, raise your energy vibrations and become one with the universe.

Creative Manifestation

Write it down:

The act of writing starts transforming your goal from a dream into a physical reality.

- Keep it simple
- Make it specific
- Write it in present tense as if you have it now
- Use positive language.

Visualize it:

- Create pictures of having it now
- Hold a clear picture of the end result in the mind.

Accept it:

- Leave the 'how' to the universe
- Believe 100 percent you will get it
- Flow with the river of life
- Let go of the importance of it, of any self-investment
- Take inspired action
- Act as if you have it NOW.

Be grateful for it:

- Say thank you as if you already have it: gratitude attracts more good to you
- Remember that appreciation makes more. Depreciation makes less
- Be generous.

Powerful Visualizations

With a specific goal written down, engage your unconscious mind, your emotional mind, with a powerful visualization of the end result. We visualize only the final outcome, the end result, so that we don't get caught up in the how of it. Leave the how to your magical mind, your creative unconscious mind, which can bring things about in ways you cannot imagine.

The following powerful visualization process activates mental pictures, sounds and feelings and in this way excites, motivates and mobilizes your unconscious mind:

What is the last thing that needs to happen for you to know you've achieved your goal? How will you know you've achieved it?

> What do you see?
>
> Where are you?
>
> Who else is there?
>
> What are they saying to you?
>
> What are you saying to yourself?
>
> What else do you hear?
>
> How good does it feel, having achieved this?

Now step into your picture, look through your own eyes.

What do you see around you?

Add some colour to make it even more compelling.

If you made your picture brighter, clearer, bigger, bolder, nearer, would it be more compelling? Play with it, Photoshop it.

> What do you hear?
>
> Turn up the volume and improve the sound's clarity.

What are you saying to yourself?

What are others saying to you?

Hear it clearly.

What are you feeling?

Really turn up the intensity of those feelings; enjoy feeling those feelings.

Now, despite how good it feels to be in the picture, step out of it. Look at yourself in your picture.

How are you different now that you have achieved your goal?

What are you wearing?

What is the expression on your face?

What's your posture?

How are you standing, sitting, walking, carrying yourself?

Put a frame around your picture.

Now that you are clear about your desired end result, you can take your picture, your vision, into the manifestation meditation.

Manifestation Meditation

Meditation to shift into the heart and manifest your desired outcomes

Manifesting the fifth-dimensional way activates heart-based consciousness.

Relax, become aware of your breathing.

Become aware of your body. Spend a moment in gratitude for the body, for all its automatic processes, for your unconscious mind running your body, keeping you energized and healthy, naturally.

Relax the body. Who are you beyond the body?

Become aware of your feelings, your emotions. How are you feeling now?

Now shift beyond these feelings. Who are you beyond your feelings?

Shift your awareness into the heart.

Take your consciousness into the heart.

Breathe into the heart.

Hear and feel your heartbeat.

Begin to relax the heart area; feel it becoming warm as you open your heart. Spread that warmth through the body.

Your heart is the gateway to the formless aether, the world of energy where everything is still only a wave of potentiality and creativity. Your heart is the centre of your intuition, where your inspiration and ideas come from when you are relaxed. When you are relaxed, your imagination opens up and you can be infinitely creative. Your heart is the centre of love, joy and peace. Love really starts with self-love. Spend a few moments loving, appreciating and being grateful for who you are. You are totally unique and immensely valuable. Your life has a special purpose, one that only you can fulfill.

Say to yourself:

My body is relaxed.

My heart is at peace.

My mind is calm.

My mind is in the service of my heart.

I am at peace. All is well.

Settle in the present moment, in the heart

Allow your awareness to expand beyond yourself.

Wider and wider, fill the room with your energy, your awareness. Expand your awareness beyond the room, wider and wider into the nothingness – beyond the planet, beyond the solar system into the wider universe, into the void. Notice it's all one thing with which you are one.

You are entering a state of unity consciousness, a state of oneness with everyone and everything, where everything is pure energy, pure light. The fifth dimension. Here, everything is still a wave of potential.

Here, you are connected to the source of life, your source of energy and good health.

Here you are your higher self, your true self. You are pure spirit, a being of light. You are pure energy. Your essential nature is love, joy and happiness.

Here you have access to abundant resources.

Here you are the creator of your universe.

Your higher self is the source of magic and miracles, prosperity, happiness and perfect health.

Now, see your dream manifestation, that picture of your imagined goal.

Take your vision, your framed picture, and drop it into the quantum pool of energy, and as you do, all that you need to manifest your dream will come to you, just at the right moment.

See the ripples going out from the pool of nothingness to the world of form, all the way to you, perfect cause and effect, perfect creation.

Now let it go in good faith and trust; it is done.

Give thanks for all that you already have and for all the magic and miracles that are still coming your way.

Now, simply because you have placed your intention right there into the fifth-dimensional world of energy, potentiality, perfection, and interconnectedness of everything, the whole universe is already conspiring to arrange for you what you want. The universe is working through people, circumstances and synchronized events to help you achieve what you want. This is what the universe does, what your higher self does – naturally, by the universal laws.

As you slowly bring yourself back to the world of form, follow the ripples and know that at some level, what you want already exists for you.

As you bring yourself back to the world of form, do so with the intention of staying in this magical mode of being – relaxed and yet full of life, energized and in a state of expanded awareness, with excitement and creative energy flowing through you.

Ground yourself back in the body, in the here and now.

Visit *http://liftingtheveilsofillusion.co.uk/meditations/* to download a free audio meditation: Shifting into the heart and manifesting your desired outcomes.

Journey through the Chakras: Third Chakra Contemplation and Visualization

Chakra	Third chakra: the solar chakra, above the navel
Function	Personal power, healthy ego, self-worth, passion, freedom of choice, individuality, self-esteem, boundaries, immunity, digestion
Emotion	Anger
Colour	Yellow
Spiritual Law	Honour oneself
Meditation	I can
Element	Fire
Crystal	Citrine, tiger eye, yellow calcite, topaz

The solar plexus is just above the navel and below the ribcage. The name implies the sun within. Here is where you become aware of your sense of identity; your unique personality. It is the centre of your personal power, confidence and self-esteem. Its colour is yellow and the element is fire. Visualize bringing in the warm energy of yellow sunlight; feel the fire within. This fire can be the spark of new initiative, enthusiasm and drive. It can also be the fire that fuels anger. Anger in its healthy form is assertiveness – an essential boundary energy. Here we come into our own right, honouring ourselves as unique individuals, separated from the tribe. This is a centre of transformation. The fire burns off the excess emotions of the watery sacral chakra. Visualize bright yellow sunlight within. Feel your inner power, passion and spontaneity – the confidence to make decisions and be your own individual self. Stand in your own power so that you can be the powerful creator of your own life.

Soul Laundry

Left-brained life stress stress stress
Could there be anything else?

Go online, find Narina's site
I'm seeking to bring in more of the light

Meditation, me time, time to chill
De-stress, unwind without a pill

What's under the veil? I'm curious to see
Will I discover more about me?

Personal responsibility, take control
Ready to evolve this wounded soul

I flow with life, leave behind the strife and clear
the clutter from my life

I'm not that person who used to cower
It's time for confidence, boundaries, standing in my power

Energies, healing, more clutter gone, move up a
chakra & start again

What will arise? Pull down that veil
Progression slowed down to the speed of a snail

Increase my vibrations, it's all kicked off again
Time to come out of my comfortable den

Cut those cords, energy returned
Release those times that I've been burned

I speak my truth, free to be me
There is only love, it's now clear to see

Cleanse, detox, purify and the opening up of my third eye!

Decalcify pineal, connect to the truth
High vibrations going through the roof

Crown chakra & my connection to Spirit
and the realisation, there are no limits

BY GEMMA DRAPER
CHAKRA HOLISTICS

Step 4: Loving Unconditionally

Illusion 4	We are separate
Reality	We are all one – interconnected
Shift	Practise unconditional love, compassion and forgiveness *Remember:* What I do to others, I do to myself What I think of others, I think of myself I see in others who I am
Healing Meditation	Heal relationships, forgive, reconnect

Forgiveness, Transcendence and Unconditional Love

The fourth veil dissolves when you hold unconditional love in your heart for everyone and everything. Doing so often involves deep forgiveness; often a shift in consciousness; it involves changing your perceptions of those testing people in your life, and those who caused you hurt. This changed perception is based on the idea that, from a higher perspective, all is for the greater good. It involves seeing with divine eyes; seeing that everything is in agreement. Even before we came into this world we co-created our life purpose with divine guidance, and it includes many agreements to meet and work with certain people in certain places at certain times. To help you learn the lesson you want to learn, others agreed to act out certain roles (Schwartz, 2012). Their actions are those of love, however much disguised they may be.

'All the world's a stage, and all the men and women merely players'.
- WILLIAM SHAKESPEARE

The people in our lives are our teachers. We grow and evolve through relationships.

'Forgiving and releasing old hurts from your system is like taking a mental and emotional bath', says HeartMath founder Doc Childre. 'To forgive, you need to dislodge your judgements even before you fully understand why things happened, but most people want to understand why someone "wronged" them before they forgive. It's a Catch-22 situation.'[2]

Forgiveness is essential for your health. You heal yourself when you forgive. Louise Hay followed a healthy lifestyle to cure her cancer. It was when she finally forgave her parents for her violent childhood that she was able to heal. Dr Wayne Dyer turned hatred towards his father for abandoning the family into forgiveness, to find peace. 'It was a moment of forgiveness that turned my whole life around. Forgiveness is really an act of letting go, releasing the anger, the hatred, the bitterness, the thoughts of revenge that we have been carrying around. We can do this letting go without even encountering the person we want to forgive', he says.[3]

Research has shown how anger, resentment and hostility physically affect the heart – these emotions can cause hardening of the arteries and heart attacks (Edwards, 2010). Forgiveness doesn't mean condoning the behaviour of a person who has hurt you, nor does it mean you cannot express how you feel or assert healthy

---

2. https://www.heartmath.org/articles-of-the-heart/heartmath-tools-techniques/ be-healthy-and-happy-forgive/
3. http://www.drwaynedyer.com/blog/category/forgiveness/

boundaries to prevent any further wrongdoing. As Jack Kornfield (2002) reminds us, we have all been wronged and we have all caused suffering to others. When we let go of the blame, compassion can enter the heart and set us free.

Forgiveness allows you to ascend on the ladder of emotional levels, described in Step 2. The Mayan prophecies on entering a new era of enlightenment say that those who have their relationships in order will go through more easily (Benedict, 2008). More on this in the Epilogue.

There is only one true emotion and that is love. Unconditional love doesn't always come easily. It's easy to love your child unconditionally regardless of his or her behaviour. However, it's not always as easy with those testing people in our lives. We can make unconditional love an intentional spiritual practice. As you practise it, the heart centre opens and then it becomes your nature.

At the heart centre we transcend form as we go beyond the ego into the true higher self. This involves integrating the self-centred intentions of the ego self with that of the higher self, whose intentions are for a greater purpose and for the greater good.

Useful and empowering beliefs for healthy, happy relationships

1. **Cause > Effect (as described in Step 1)** –
   shift any victim mindset to an awareness of the cause.
   Take 100 percent responsibility for your own feelings and needs.

2. **Your relationships with others mirror your primary relationship** – with yourself.

3. **Every relationship has one key purpose** –
   to help you learn about yourself.

---

4. **We attract people to us according to how we are** – when you see yourself as worthy of love and appreciation, those around you will act accordingly.

5. **We can only change ourselves** – we cannot change others – and when we change, everything changes.

6. **Everyone is equal in value.**

7. **Separateness is an illusion** – we are all one (like waves in the ocean).

8. **Your unconscious mind takes everything personally, including what you say about others** – point a finger and three fingers point back!

9. **True love begins with self-love.**

10. **Our view of reality is only a perception (as described in Step 1)** –

    • Everything that we perceive outside of us is a projection from inside of us

    • We project our perceptions onto others

    • What you see in others is who you are yourself (what you like and don't like)

    • Everyone is a mirror of an aspect of you; you are always looking in a mirror

    • When you change your perceptions, everything and everyone around you changes

    • Everyone is your teacher, helping you to learn something about yourself – especially those who press your buttons!

    • Whatever you think you are, you are always more than that. You are a magnificent and all-powerful being of light with infinite potential to change, and so is everyone else.

*'Be the change you want to see
in the world'.*
- GANDHI

Equally, be the friend you want to have; give the love you want to receive. You must also forgive yourself. We often give ourselves a hard time through criticism, blame and unreasonable demands. Love is divine power. Remember, love really starts with self-love. You can only extend the quantity and quality of love that you feel for yourself. Caroline Myss refers to two spiritual laws that we are to bring in balance here: honouring one another and honouring yourself (Myss, 1996). The misconception that it's right to put other people first can lead to resentment. No one is more important than anyone else. Energetic imbalances can leave you feeling drained. Balancing these principles means honouring ourselves *as* we honour one another. We are all equal in value.

Making Peace

It's best for your own healing to be at peace with everyone in your life. You don't have to necessarily like everyone, and there will certainly be people you won't want to spend a lot of time with and that's all right – as long as you are at peace in your own heart for your own sake. The ancient people of Hawaii knew the importance of forgiveness in regards to healing. They achieved forgiveness through the wonderful practice of *ho'oponopono*, which has in recent years become more mainstream in Western society. *Ho'oponopono* means 'to make right'; 'to make rightly right' (Dupree, 2012). The Hawaiians had a great understanding of energy. They believed that we carry everyone we ever connected with inside us as part of us. When we are with another person, we connect to him or her energetically through the auras. Connections are made through touch, sex, strong emotions (even anger and upset), strong thoughts, and any communication (even on the phone). This connection, according to the Hawaiians, is made by means of an aka cord. Aka is a sticky substance in the aura that keeps us connected, even after parting, and that opens a flow of energy between people. If you have many such connections open, your energy can feel scattered. This means your energy is leaking; flowing out to others without a purpose. You are supplying them with your energy. Also, emotional wounds, negative emotions, blame and regrets keep us in the past. Dwelling on the past encourages depression. If you still feel angry with your ex, the negative emotions keep you energetically attached to him or her. That's why the person remains on your mind. As long as we think of a relationship with resentment, hatred, sadness or disappointment, we will attract similar relationships through the resonance principle, or generally block ourselves off from harmonious and loving relationships (Dupree, 2012). Forgiveness restores your energy and your health and sets you free. It can feel as though a huge weight is lifting off your shoulders as you put the past behind you peacefully.

Meditation: Ho'oponopono – Cutting Connections

An exercise in forgiveness, healing and peacemaking

This meditation serves as telepathic communication within the collective unconscious mind – higher self to higher self. At this level, forgiveness comes more easily. The result is miraculous: old energy is cleared and the slate is literally wiped clean.

You choose whom you want to cut yourself from. When you do this meditation for the first time, it's best to cut from everyone to clear your energy of past connections. You can always reconnect again, and when you do, they will experience you for who you are at present, free from the past. People's opinions of who you used to be can keep you stuck. Therefore, as you cut the connections, you can stand in your own true light and be seen for who you truly are. This process is based on your projected perceptions and is therefore a great way to manage your perceptions as well.

Results of the Ho'oponopono meditation

1. **Healing** – physical, emotional and spiritual

2. **Forgiveness** – of self and others, which leads to liberation and a miraculous transition to a higher level of consciousness

3. **Clean slate** – an official new beginning

4. **Energy retrieval** – bringing energy back into integrity.

Process

1. **Imagine you are in a place of no time and infinite space.**

2. **Create a platform in your mind onto which you can invite people you want to cut from energetically.**

3. **Start the healing process.**
   Connect with Source, with the light. See yourself in a source of light; an infinite source of love and healing.
   Take this healing light into all of your being.
   See yourself becoming lighter and brighter.
   Feel the warmth and love of this healing light.
   Fill yourself up to overflow.
   Then channel this infinite source of love and healing onto the platform to facilitate the healing of those you are going to call up.

4. **Keep allowing the infinite source of love and healing to flow through you onto the platform.**

5. **Invite people onto your platform.**
   You might want to invite parents, grandparents, brothers, sisters, uncles, aunts, children, nephews, nieces, friends (old and new), colleagues, clients, teachers, mentors, students, partners, ex-partners, neighbours – anyone your unconscious mind brings up.

6. **Have a discussion with these people in your mind, individually or as a group, clearing any issues.**

7. **Say: 'I'm sorry, please forgive me. I love you.
Do you love me? Do you forgive me?'**
Hear and feel the forgiveness.
When the forgiveness is done, thank them.
The aka cords will dissolve and the people will
float off the platform, becoming one with the light.
Remember, the people on the platform are only your
projections, so the forgiveness is really up to you.
Besides, it's for your own healing.
You will know it's done when inner peace
and harmony return.

8. **When the platform is clear, it represents your
clean slate, your official new beginning.**
This is the wonder of life: you can always start again.
Every day can be a new beginning.

9. **As you forgive and let go, you become whole again.**
This is healing and ultimately you are your own healer.

10. **Ground back into the body.**

Visit *http://liftingtheveilsofillusion.co.uk/meditations/* to download
a free audio meditation: *Ho'oponopono: Cutting connections and
healing relationships.*

Journey through the Chakras: Fourth Chakra Contemplation and Visualization

Chakra	Fourth chakra: the heart chakra, in the centre of the chest
Function	Love, compassion, acceptance, peace, caring, healing through forgiveness
Emotion	Hurt, upset, love
Colour	Green (and pink for higher heart)
Spiritual Law	Love is divine power

Meditation	I love
Element	Air
Crystal	Peridot, malachite, rose quartz, green jade, green aventurine

The heart chakra, the centre of our bodies, binds the physical and spiritual centres. It unites Heaven and Earth in the body. Here we are reborn into the light. Having established and fulfilled a healthy ego at the level of the third chakra, we have a sound foundation from which to transcend the ego and become our true authentic selves; a foundation from which to transform from personal to universal. Here we start our spiritual journey by cultivating harmony, compassion and unconditional love – these are the qualities of the heart. Divine love seeks nothing in return. The heart chakra's element is air, which can be gentle or stormy as it brings change, transforming anger into love, forgiveness and compassion. Breathe deeply into this centre and feel the cleansing, expansive quality of the air. Visualize a harmonious green colour in your chest. This centre of love is first and foremost about self-love. Self-love is a powerful healer. Self-love is the foundation of good health and happiness. Visualize this chakra opening, unfolding like new green leaves, or see it as a bright emerald, a beautiful gem shining in your heart. The heart chakra is also linked to the hand chakras (minor chakras in the palms of your hands), through which we reach out to touch, love and heal others. Here we also pause and give thanks for all the abundance of the universe. Gratitude welcomes abundance into our lives.

An Experience of Forgiveness

During the last twelve months of working alongside Narina my awareness has been drawn more and more towards the theme of forgiveness, as a key to both personal healing and that of humanity.

I was introduced to the Ho'oponopono prayer by a wonderfully inspiring 80-year-old lady; with many years of practising forgiveness. I sat-up and took notice.

The Ho'oponopono is the Hawaiian ritual of forgiveness, when there is a desire to solve conflict and problems. The premise is unity in everything, even though we feel ourselves to be separated. Because of unity or oneness, nothing can happen in our world without it resonating in the observer. If we change our inner resonance to one of forgiveness, it resonates in the observer, promoting unity, harmony and inner peace. The very opposite would be true of anger.

To accomplish this resonance between the forgiver and the receiver, the Ho'oponopono relies on four simple yet powerful statements:

I am sorry.

Please forgive me.

I love you.

Thank you.

Ho'oponopono helps us to shift the way we think or perceive a situation. It works like an affirmation. Forgiveness releases and empowers us.

I have experienced some remarkable changes in both my own and other people's attitudes when working with the Ho'oponopono.

My dog Dillon and I were taking our usual morning walk. We cut across the village playing field with Dillon off his lead. In the distance I spotted a gentleman with a dog on a lead and two young girls, making their way across the field to the public footpath that leads to the village school.

I made to put Dillon on the lead to stop him from running over to meet and greet! I was seconds too late, off he shot. Dillon completely ignored my calls to return to me. As the group advanced without stopping Dillon continued in his pursuit, running round and round the family group.

Several times I politely asked the gentleman to simply stop to allow me to catch Dillon. He flatly refused, saying he was late, stubbornly marching on and shouting at me that I should have the dog under control. I was completely in agreement with him, but his lack of cooperation was only escalating the situation, causing the girls stress and holding them up. Finally he stopped, allowing me to catch Dillon.

I was left shaking and distressed by the aggressive and unreasonable behaviour of the gentleman.

Not wanting to perpetuate my feelings of disharmony I used the Ho'oponopono, I repeated the prayer on numerous occasions sending out the intention of forgiveness towards the gentleman. Eventually I felt at peace with the occurrence and the gentleman. However, I was unable to walk that way again for fear of meeting him. The incident had prompted me to undertake some private dog-training sessions enabling me to bring Dillon under greater control.

To my surprise a few weeks later the very same gentleman stopped me, saying he had been looking out for me as he wanted to apologise for his behaviour. He said that he had been stressed and reacted badly. He said that he could not retract his statement that I should be able to control my dog, but he regretted the way he had spoken to me. I thanked him for his apology saying how much I appreciated his candidness.

BY JOSEPHINE ORMEROD

Forgiveness is not an occasional act,
it is a constant attitude.
- DR. MARTIN LUTHER KING

Love, Life and Joy

True Love is a magical gift
To do to share and to receive

The warm glow
The inner and sometimes outer smile it brings

These moments they are like treasures
More precious than anything on this earth
Because they stay with you forever

The purest of love is when it is given and received
Without any need or expectation in return

Honour and grace in giving and receiving love
Are qualities that provide the richness beyond our wildest dreams

The art is to allow our hearts to be open to the possibilities
The depth to which we can reach is endless

How do we start you may ask?

We come to our hearts
Be our truest selves
… and breathe deeply

– BY JULIE SWIFT
TAI CHI, CHI KUNG AND ENERGY PRACTITIONER

Step 5: Reconnecting with Nature

Illusion 5	Only humans have consciousness
Reality	Everything is interconnected We are all one with nature, made of the same elements – the web of life Consciousness is in everything: the planet, plants, animals Through connection and balance you create your own health
Shift	Return to nature; live in harmony with its cycles
Ritual Meditation	Honour the elements and natural cycles

Everything is Interconnected: the Web of Life

The fifth veil dissolves when you experience the interconnectedness of everything and restore your connections with nature. Nature's energy vibrates at a high level and has a therapeutic, restorative healing effect on us. We are integrally part of nature. The cycles of the seasons, the moon and the planets have profound effects on us. We are made of the same substance as nature – the same elements of air, fire, water and earth. Nature is constantly flowing through us as we breathe, drink water, eat food and soak up warmth. We can heal ourselves by balancing the elements in our own bodies. Getting out in nature can give us an instant sense of relief, relaxation and freedom. We are nature. We are related to everything. This is the web of life. Everything is connected and interrelated. Consciousness is in every living and inanimate thing.

Over the years we have lost our connection with our natural home. Modern-day cosmopolitan life separates us from nature as we spend many busy hours in traffic, in offices, in homes and in our minds; we are stressed out, anxious, depressed and ill. Our chase after material things results in pollution and exploitation of natural resources. These are the last remnants of our out-dated values; the end of an outgoing era.

Time to Return to Nature

Fortunately, something is happening all over the world. It's as if Mother Nature is calling us to reconnect. We are awakening from our illusion of separateness. Sustainability has become an accepted government policy. Simple living and minimalism is becoming more appealing. People are buying more vegetable plants at garden centres and growing their own food. People are more mindful of what's on their plates, of where and how their food was grown. We are reading labels, demanding fairness and honesty from the consumer market, taking responsibility for our own health. Growing food helps us tune in to natural cycles.

The Mayan prophesies on the new world age and the shift in human consciousness predicted this return to nature and its cycles (Benedict, 2008).

As we bring our awareness back to the wonder of the natural world, we quickly realize our fundamental interconnectedness. Everything is one and we are part of something much greater than us. 'Bringing our awareness back to nature lies at the heart of our happiness and of the well-being of all life on Earth' (Thompson, 2013).

Returning to nature also means simply being in our bodies. Our bodies are our natural home, our gift of nature. As we accelerate into higher levels of consciousness, it will become even more important to remain grounded in the body. Grounding practices such as spending time in nature, gardening, cooking, and eating root vegetables and grains can restore balance.

Being mindful of the natural world by giving it your full attention, experiencing it with all your senses, opens you up to a magical world just under your nose and too often unnoticed. The busy mind can separate us from our direct experience of life. Mindfulness practices in nature clear the chatter of the thinking mind, restore calm and give you a sense of well-being, of being truly alive, in the moment. It is thanks to our senses that we are able to experience life to the fullest.

'Look deep into nature,
and then you'll understand everything
better'.
- ALBERT EINSTEIN

In the book *Earthing* (2010), Ober, Sinatra and Zucker describe the natural healing benefits of walking barefoot, in direct contact with the earth. Earth's surface is alive with electrical energy that is continuously replenished by the sun and by lightning activity. The sole of the foot has 1300 nerve endings designed to keep us in touch with the earth and to draw vital energy for nourishment and good health. Modern buildings – homes and offices – are elevated and constructed with nonconductive material, separating us from the earth's healing electrons. Our shoes, too, are made from plastic, rubber and other nonconductive material, separating us further from the energy of and sensory connection with the earth. The simple practice of walking barefoot has striking, even transformational, effects on people's health and vitality. The authors quote numerous examples of inflammatory-related disorders, fatigue, insomnia and chronic pain being relieved or even vanishing as a result.

Nature has built-in intelligence, and since everything is interlinked and connected, we may also wish to turn to nature to restore our immune systems.

Elements: the Building Blocks of Life

The five essential elements are the building blocks that all life forms contain: aether, air, fire, water and earth. We can see how life was created from the subtlest to the grossest matter. From eternity, the subtlest form of matter is aether – the void, the quantum space. Aether mixed with eternity creates air, a more observable or experiential element. As air moves, it eventually creates friction, which in turn creates heat or fire. Heat produces moisture, thus creating water, a denser element yet. If one tries to walk through water, one is slowed by its density. Finally, water produces the densest form of matter – earth. The Vedas – the earliest body of Indian scripture – say that all of creation, including humans, is made up of combinations of all five essential elements. These elements are the subtlest aspects of human life, finer than the molecular, atomic, or subatomic.

'As above, so below'
– ANCIENT HERMETIC MAXIM

As creation takes place in the macrocosm, so it does in the microcosm. We too create everything in our lives, first with a thought, an idea (air) that stirs up passion and drive (fire) and moves us to take inspired, creative action (water) that eventually results in a tangible outcome (earth).

Energy Is All There Is

How are you created energetically?

Apart from your physical body, your energy field, or aura, consists of your subtle energy bodies, namely your emotional body, your mental body and your spiritual body. Your four bodies are linked with the elements of fire, air, water and earth (see 'The body and its auric field' illustration below). The fifth element is aether, the unifying element – in the field of the quantum physicist. These five elements form the basis of all energy healing, and working with the elements can bring you back into balance and good health.

Achieving balance, health and well-being through the elements is an ancient philosophy still practised in Ayurveda. 'Ayurveda is a 5,000-year-old system of natural healing that has its origins in the Vedic culture of India. Ayurveda has been enjoying a major resurgence in both its native land and throughout the world. Tibetan Medicine and Traditional Chinese Medicine both have their roots in Ayurveda. Early Greek medicine also embraced many concepts originally described in the classical Ayurvedic medical texts dating back thousands of years. Recognising that human beings are part of nature, Ayurveda reminds us that health is the balanced and dynamic integration between our environment, body, mind, and spirit' (The Chopra Centre). Elemental work forms the basis of many other ancient spiritual and healing systems such as alchemy and Taoism with its tai chi and chi kung practices. Disease is an imbalance of the five elements in the body. Through connection and balance we can create and maintain our own health. A good understanding of the differences in vibration between the five elements will empower you to self-heal. The finer vibrations of fire and aether take us to spirit while the earth element grounds us in the body and connects us to the earth.

'Your body is designed to heal itself.
The ability of the body to maintain its health
and overcome illness is, in fact,
among nature's most remarkable feats'.
- DONNA EDEN

The elements are physical and metaphysical. So whether we take in the actual physical element or work with it energetically (e.g., through energy work like tai chi or yoga or through visualization or imagination), the effect is the same. The unconscious mind doesn't distinguish between reality and imagination. For example, we can take in the element of fire by physically being outside, soaking up the sunshine, and by doing physical exercise to generate warmth and energy in the body. Metaphysically we can visualize the sun and its purifying effect within. Equally, we can ground ourselves through physical contact with the earth or by visualizing ourselves rooted into the earth.

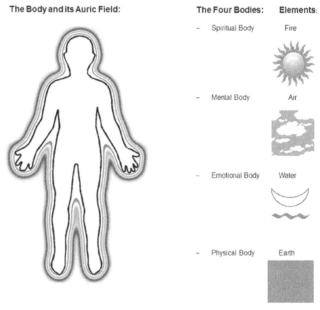

'The body and its auric field'

Working with the Elements for Balance and Healing

Aether

Aether is formlessness, the nothing, the seed, the space from which all creation arises. This is the space of the quantum physicist; the space that allows for movement. Aether is beyond our concept of time and space. It is pure spirit, pure energy, pure potentiality. Aether pervades everything. It is the unifying element from which the other four elements arise. Aether is the trance element and can be useful for hypnosis and meditation. It is the vehicle for thought transfer and telepathy. Generate aether by decluttering and giving yourself some space.

> **Chakra:** Throat chakra and up
>
> **Symbol:** Oval
>
> **Colour:** Dark purple
>
> **Sound:** *Ham; ohm,* or *IAO (eeeeeeaaaaaaooooo)*
>
> **Movement:** In energy work such as tai chi, you can activate aether by imagining painting a rainbow bridge around you with a circular arm movement while seeing yourself within a rainbow light.

Visualize a dark purple oval to bring in the element of aether; e.g., when you want to deepen your meditative state.

Air

Air is essentially movement. Movement begins the creation process. Yang, masculine in nature, this element rules the mental plane, the mental body, your thought processes. Air brings mental clarity. Air balances fire and water. Generate this element through breathing practices and going out for a breath of fresh air.

Chakra: Heart chakra

Symbol: Circle

Colour: Sky blue

Sound: *Yam; HA* (an audible, lengthened out-breath: 1-to-2-ratio breathing)

Movement: In tai chi, the element of air is created by a movement called Waving the Hands like the Clouds. The arms and hands create circular movements past the forehead as if wiping thoughts away. This movement works in the auric field and clears the mind of thoughts.

Visualize floating clouds in a clear blue sky to connect with the air element; e.g., to stimulate clear thinking.

Fire

The first spark of creation, fire is electric. Yang, masculine in nature, this element rules the spiritual body. Fire is expansive and radiates outward. Fire is expressive and aggressive in taking action. The element of fire provides us with the passion, drive, motivation and will to take action. Focus is an electrical current that energizes what we want to bring about. Fire brings change and transformation. The body needs fire for good vision and healthy digestion. Generate this element through exercise, warming foods, spending time in the sun, sitting by a fire or lighting a candle.

Chakra: Solar plexus (sun within)

Symbol: Triangle or the sun

Colour: Red or gold like the sun

Sound: *Ram; Ssshhh* (the in-breath and out-breath are short and sharp: 1-to-1 ratio breathing)

Movement: During energy work, to generate fire in the body, start in the horse-riding stance, knees bent. Visualize the sun directly overhead and cup your hands, then imagine grabbing sunlight and pushing it down with a quick movement while doing the fire breath, *ssshhh*. This rapidly increases the energy, so do four breaths at a time and take a breather in between.

Visualize the sun in the solar plexus for energy and good health.

Water

Water rules the emotional plane, your emotional body, your feelings. Yin, feminine in nature, this element is nurturing, caring, calming and relaxing. Where fire is electric and expansive, water is magnetic and contractive. Water attracts and draws energy inward. Water is cooling and promotes fluidity and flexibility. Intention (information, desire) is magnetic and attracts to you what you want to bring about. Balance the water element in you by healing and releasing emotions. Spending time near water and swimming and showering mindfully will connect you to the restorative, calming effect of the water element.

Chakra: Sacral chakra

Symbol: Silver crescent moon

Colour: Deep ocean blue and silvery moon

Sound: *Vam*; *Mmmmm* (1-to-2-ratio breathing)

Movement: Practise the tai chi movement called Pushing the Ocean Waves. Visualize standing in a lake or a deep blue ocean lit by a reflective crescent moon. With one foot slightly in front of the other, gather water in and push the waves out, washing water through the lower centres to clear and cleanse. Change feet halfway through.

Visualize a crescent moon reflecting on a deep blue ocean or dark lake.

Earth

Earth rules the physical plane, your physical body, your physical health. The earth element represents form – manifested creation. Yin, feminine in nature, this element is cooling and nurturing, solid and dense. The element of earth provides stability, support and strength and keeps us grounded – connected to the earth. Earth brings structure and slows and stabilizes energy to manifest abundance. Cultivate grounding and connection with this element through attention to the physical body, exercise, walking in nature, and eating protein, root vegetables and whole grains.

Chakra: Root chakra

Symbol: Square

Colour: Yellow/brown

Sound: *Lam*; *HAW* (a throat-clearing sound, useful for grounding)

Movement: Raise and ground your energy. In a horse-riding stance, rooted, raise the energy with a hand-lifting movement, taken from the ground up to above your knees, and then push it down over the knees to ground the energy. Stomping is also a great grounding practice.

Visualise yourself rooted to the earth. Imagine roots like the roots of a tree connecting your feet with the earth and penetrating deep into the earth.

THE QUALITIES OF THE FIVE ELEMENTS	
Aether	Unifying element, the field of the quantum physicist: pure spirit, pure energy, the unseen, nothing, space Too much: spacey, lacking presence, disconnected Too little: overwhelmed, lacking a sense of time and space
Air	Mind: ideas, thought, clarity, movement, love, compassion; yang Too much: airheaded, spacey, restless Too little: stuck for ideas
Fire	Spirit: transformation, inspiration, passion, enthusiasm, joy, excitement, motivation, drive, intuition; yang Too much: angry, intense, impatient, feverish Too little: cold; tendency to procrastinate; lack willpower and direction; digestive problems, eyesight problems
Water	Emotions: feelings, nurturing, calm; yin Too much: teary, overly sensitive; self-pitying; retaining water Too little: detached from feelings; unable to express affection; uncomfortable around others
Earth	Body: form, health, grounding, safety, stability, abundance; yin Too much: materialistic, lethargic, lazy, dull, rigid, inflexible, stuck; resisting change Too little: flighty, spacey, agitated, ungrounded, unstable, unreliable; lacking in sexual drive; a racing mind; great ideas unable to be manifested

The Elements and Life

*Life is sustained by the elemental forces and
the elemental forces sustain life.
This circle is a natural law influencing all life on earth.*

*The elements of earth, water, fire, air and ether make up this world.
The planet and all its creatures and plants depend on
a healthy balance of these elements.
Sustaining each element is a pattern of elemental energy force.
This energy forms the web of life, the inter-connectedness of all things.
Energy weaves together the whole moving from the unseen to the seen.
Un-manifest to manifest.*

*__Earth__ the bones give physical form
The structure, foundation for life
Experienced through the senses
Touch, taste, smell, vision
Be strong, feel safe in the world
Relax, be still and stable
Tread the earth with confidence
Know your purpose
__Grounded in life__*

*__Water__ – blood – emotions that ebb and flow
Balanced, the emotions flow as water in the river
Contained with the natural boundaries of river bank
Practise and preserve the calm centre
The natural emotional state is calmness
Move through life with grace
Enjoying its pleasure and gifts
Nurturing yourselves and those around you
__Flow with life__*

*__Fire__ – power – vital force
Passion and energy
Like the light from the sun
The natural state is light, clear and bright*

With this lightness comes inner knowing
As the light dissolves the shadows
See more clearly
Trust your intuition
Heat of the fire warms the personality
Be confident, spontaneous, humorous and playful
Sparkle with life

Air – *thoughts rest in the mind*
Open, spacious and free
The natural state of mind is light, mobile and clear
The imagination opens easily
Thoughts moving like clouds blown on a
Gentle breeze in a blue sky
Allow the mind to be calm
At the heart inner stillness
Connect with the higher creative forces
Love, compassion, empathy and peace
Lighten to life

Aether – *in the space the spirit dwells*
Perfect, subtle, spacious mind
All the elements fused as one
In the centre of the soul
The web of Universal/Divine consciousness
Manifest on the earth
Open to Spaciousness

Truth – Knowing – Light
Om Mani Padme Hum

BY SUE KEADY
OWNER OF THE TOWNGATE COMPLEMENTARY THERAPY CLINIC,
ACUPUNCTURIST AND TAI CHI TEACHER

Meditation: Loving Kindness and Healing Meditations for Seasons and Cycles

Practise a mindfulness walking meditation to clear the mind and reconnect. Make the birds' sounds your single point of mindfulness, or simply sit with nature.

In springtime

Sit under a fruit tree (or imagine you are doing so). It's springtime and the tree is in full bloom. As you look up through its branches, consider the seasons: how they change, how nature changes. Consider the impermanence of everything – a time for blossoms, a time for leaves, a time for fruit, a time for leaves to fall, a time to let go, a time to rest, a time to hibernate and be still.

Notice the bees busy among the blossoms. Consider nature's wonderful design, how the fruit trees depend on the bees for pollination and fruit. Everything is interconnected – the magical web of life. There's a time for everything. How can you embrace this energy of spring? A time of new beginnings, abundant energy, new ideas and initiatives.

Become aware of all the elements: Feel your connection with the earth beneath your feet – breathe in the air, feel the warmth of the sun, see how the tree uses water to produce flowers and fruit. Feel respect and gratitude for the things in nature we depend on: air, water, energy and food – all gifts of nature.

> Loving kindness to yourself:
> Feel your own heartbeat.
> Accept and appreciate everything just as it is, right now.
> Repeat this phrase to yourself, like a mantra:
> *May I be happy, may I be well.*

Bring any thoughts into your awareness as you come back into your heart area:
May I be happy, may I be well.

Loving kindness to others:
Bring to mind those special people close to you:
May they be happy, may they be well.

Also bring to mind those people you may find a little more testing. Become aware that they too have their own challenges and they too want to be happy and well.
May they be happy, may they be well.

Loving kindness to all living things:
Extend the feeling of loving kindness to all living things: birds, animals, insects, plants.
They too want to be safe and free.
May they be happy, may they be well.

Loving kindness to our planet:
May the planet be happy, may the planet be well.

Loving kindness to the universe:
May all the planets, stars and galaxies be happy, may the universe be well.

Notice the web of life – how everything is interconnected and interdependent; the cycles of nature, the grand design of life, of which you are a part.

Continue your reflection.

Ground back into the body: Visualize roots in the earth, like a tree, solid, grounded, connected.

In autumn

Sit beneath a big old tree (or imagine you are doing so), lean back against the trunk, feel the upward movement of the energy in the trunk opening all your energy centres. Watch the leaves fall. Notice the tree is not holding onto the leaves, nor are the leaves holding onto the tree. The leaves are letting go, effortlessly. Like the tree, what do you want to let go of?

Physically (any toxins)

Emotionally (unsettling feelings)

Mentally (excessive thoughts)

Let it go; it's time to let go. Effortlessly. The intention is enough.

During full moon

Gaze on the full moon if you can, or imagine the full moon just coming up. The moon has a gentle nurturing, healing energy. Open yourself up to it. Draw down the moon's energy for your own healing and nurturing. The moon's light is reflective.

The full moon is a time of fruition – what are you grateful for?

Continue your reflection.

The full moon is a good time for a healing meditation. Bring to mind people to whom you want to send healing. Say their names and wish them well: *May they be happy, may they be well.*

Visit *http://liftingtheveilsofillusion.co.uk/meditations/* to download a free audio meditation: Loving kindness and healing meditations for seasons and cycles.

Journey through the Chakras: Fifth Chakra Contemplation and Visualization

Chakra	Fifth chakra: the throat chakra, at the neck and throat
Function	Communication, expression (of ideas and feelings), higher will, truth
Emotion	Fear-based limiting beliefs
Colour	Blue
Spiritual Law	Surrender personal will to divine will
Meditation	I speak
Element	Sound, aether (space)
Crystal	Blue lace agate, turquoise, aquamarine

The throat chakra is the centre of communication, self-expression and sound. This is the chakra that builds a bridge between us and the world around us. Through communication we connect with others and nature. Here we find our voice and express ourselves creatively. Holding back expression is a denial of your true self and can manifest as physical discomfort in the throat and thyroid. Its colour is blue – the blue of the sky or the sea. Breathe this colour into your throat and your neck area. Its element is aether and sound. Aether allows sound to vibrate and travel. Sound can be shaped into messages we communicate and harmonised into music for joy and healing. Aether is space, a blank canvas. Be creative and express yourself freely in this world. Visualize this centre opening up to allow a free flow of creative, expressive energy.

The Web of Life

In stillness
Seed lies quietly
Waiting in the cool, dark earth
An impulse stirs

A memory awakens
Roots delve deep
A green shoot pushes through
Reaching to the light

Earth, water, fire, air breathe life
Breathe in, breathe out
Unfolding naturally

The inner knowing of the seed
Expands out into form
A Sacred pattern made manifest
An expression of Love

Strong, flexible, upright
Knowing the joy and pain of growth
It endures
Moving towards perfection

Bud into flower
Flower into fruit
Fruit ripe and full

Protecting the precious seed within
Seed of knowing
Seed of potential

The same yet different
Transformed by growth
The next generation is conceived
In Love

A new beginning
The web of life continues
In stillness

BY SUE KEADY
OWNER OF THE TOWNGATE COMPLEMENTARY THERAPY CLINIC,
ACUPUNCTURIST AND TAI CHI TEACHER

Step 6: Following Intuition to Live Your Purpose

Illusion 6	I am alone; I am lost; I have no purpose
	I am faced with random events
Reality	You are divinely guided, moment by moment
	Your higher self knows your chosen purpose (which you are here to discover)
Shift	Flow with life
	Align your intentions with your higher mind
	Create with one mind, for your highest good
	Follow your intuition
Intuitive Meditation	Communicate, ask
	Connect with inner guidance

Live Your Purpose

We each have a self-chosen path; a specific purpose; one we are here to fulfil.

How do I know if I'm living my purpose? you might ask. *How do I even begin to know my purpose?*

Deepak Chopra (1994) refers to the Law of Dharma, which relates to our purpose in life. Chopra highlights the following three components of this law:

- Each of us is here to discover our higher self or spiritual self so we can express our divinity

- Expressing our unique gifts and talents. Everyone has a unique gift and a unique way of expressing it

- Service to humanity – asking: how can I help? When you combine your unique gift with your service to humanity, joy and abundance follows.

Eckhart Tolle (2005) describes our inner and outer purpose. Our inner purpose concerns *Being* and is primary. Outer purpose concerns *Doing* and is secondary. Your inner purpose is to awaken – a shift in consciousness. The two are intertwined. Your inner purpose is the foundation for fulfilling your outer purpose. Our outer purpose is establishing the new Earth – a shift in consciousness.

Buddha teaches that your purpose in life is to find your purpose and give your whole heart and soul to it.

Because it is self-chosen, there is a part of you that knows your purpose and is actually guiding you along a specific path, moment to moment. This is your guardian spirit; your higher self; the eternal you. This guidance comes subtly, through a still voice within – your intuition. Cultivating intuitive, psychic perception and following your intuition is therefore a crucial part of the spiritual path. Your subtle higher mind doesn't use a language of words. Its language is more symbolic. Tuning into the subtle symbolism and synchronicity in your life can be very useful. The universe communicates with us all the time. We just need to listen, observe and be aware.

As you sharpen your intuition, you become more able to tap into your higher guidance and follow your path and purpose.

What is Intuition?

It is the ability to read subtle clues.

It is the ability to use energy data to make decisions in the moment (Myss, 1996). Energy data comes to us through our feelings and emotions and is about the here and the now. It allows us to take action on our gut feelings.

What is it not?

It is not a prophetic ability to tell the future. It is not fear.

The Relationship between Intuition and Self-esteem

We are all intuitive. We need to cultivate the self-esteem necessary to follow through on that gut feeling (Myss, 1996). That gut feeling directs us to take action.

The more we listen to our intuitive voice, the stronger it grows. If we ignore it once too often, it tends to give up and disappear in the background.

Honouring oneself is about following your inner guidance in spite of all the opinions and advice out there. You have a unique path and only you can live your unique mission. Being your unique self implies valuing and respecting your inner guidance, knowing it's right and true for you.

The Relationship between Intuition and Emotions

Intuition is not an emotion as we know it. Your emotions do, however, serve as a gateway to your intuitive self, and by honouring and valuing your feelings you can access and sensitize your intuition. The more you attend to your emotions as subtle messages, the stronger your intuitive ability grows. This way you become more in touch with your inner guidance, and that is a priceless gift.

How Do We Distinguish Fear from Intuition?

A reliable intuition

- Conveys information neutrally, unemotionally
- Ensures something feels right in your gut
- Has a compassionate, affirming tone
- Gives crisp, clear impressions that are 'seen' first, then felt
- Conveys a detached sensation, as if you're in a theatre watching a movie.

Irrational fear

- Is highly emotionally charged
- Has cruel, demeaning or delusional content
- Conveys no gut-centred confirmation or on-target feeling
- Reflects past psychological wounds
- Diminishes focus and perspective.

Sense It inside You

Begin to value the messages that come from inside. Learn where these messages originate in the body and how fear and intuition feel different. Take stock of what makes you afraid and distinguish irrational fears from guiding intuition.

Begin to heed your intuition by taking the right action.

Another way to tell fear and intuition apart is to question whether what you are feeling makes you feel empowered or debilitated.

Intuition comes from your spirit, your heart, your authentic self, and always has a positive intent. Fear comes from ego, from your personality, and is self-created illusion. Listening to and following the guidance of your inner voice will open you up to amazing coincidences or synchronicity, bringing a touch of magic to your life.

Develop Intuition and Symbolic Sight

Intuition can be enhanced in a number of ways. The more we attend to our intuitive hunches, the stronger our intuition grows. If we disregard that little, still voice once too often, it tends to disappear into the background. Heeding your intuition is key to your spiritual growth.

1. **Stay in the moment of NOW, detached from the outcome.**

2. **Being fully present with all of your senses is a powerful practice.**

   Detach from any investment in the outcome. One of the best ways of practising present moment awareness is through mindfulness. Mindfulness is fully immersing in the experience with all your senses without judging or labelling or wanting it to be anything else.

3. **Sharpen your sense awareness.**

   Paradoxically, intuition is enhanced when you sharpen your senses. Look around your environment and go through your five main senses. What do you see, hear, smell, feel and taste? When we fine-tune the physical senses we begin to activate the extrasensory abilities; the sixth sense.

4. **Stop worrying.**

   Yet another reason to let go of fear and worry concerning a particular outcome – it's a prerequisite for opening up to finer perception. Worry causes concerns about the future and prevents us from noticing what is happening in our minds. Busyness and stress distract us and blind us to the subtle truths of the present moment.

   To unlock your intuitive ability, recognize the illusion of fear and begin to notice what is really going on around you.

5. **Clear your mind.**

Slow your mind down and stop thinking. When your mind is clear from distracting thoughts, you are more present and able to connect with the still voice within. Meditation is a great way of clearing the mind. You can continue your meditative practice even in a public place by focusing on just one thing. This will clear the mind and increase your level of awareness. Follow the peripheral vision exercise in Step 2 to practise expanded awareness. Over time, it will become much easier to slow down or stop your thoughts.

6. **Meditate.**

Your third eye is your psychic centre, the centre of inner vision and intuition, concentration and insight. You can promote inner vision by meditating on the light within. Focus on any inner display of light or colours. What you focus on you energize. As you meditate on the light, ask for guidance, for inner vision; ask to be able to perceive the truth. Follow the sixth chakra contemplation and visualization at the end of this step to meditate on the light.

7. **Interpret your dreams.**

Dreams were hugely important to Carl Jung. He felt that dreams contain archetypal imagery and may give us valuable insights. Jung felt that a dream always has an underlying idea or intention – it expresses something important that the unconscious wants to say (Snowden, 2006).

Dreams are messages that come through your unconscious mind. The symbolism is personal, and only you can determine the meaning of your dreams.

Messages are always positive, regardless of the nature of the dream. Analysing your dreams enhances symbolic sight.

Considering the dream's theme as a whole as well as its various components, ask yourself: What does this mean to me? Go with what comes up intuitively. Then consider what actions you can take to act on the message of your dream.

8. **Enhance your subtle awareness.**

This is a quick way to feel subtle energy: Rub your hands together briskly. Then, hold them a few inches apart, palms facing. Feel the tingling of energy or perhaps a magnetic pull or push between the hands. You may feel the energy's slight resistance, almost like cotton wool.

Practise feeling a willing participant's auric field by moving your hands about 4 to 12 inches away from the person's body. Can you sense the extent of their energy field? Also, look at a person's third-eye position with a softened gaze as if to look through them. Can you begin to see their subtle aetheric outline? Over time, can you begin to see more light? The more you practise the easier it gets.

Esoteric Teachings Offer Valuable Life-purpose Tools

Sound is creation. Every sound, letter and name has a unique vibration. In the beginning there was the Word and all things in the universe were created by the Word. As above so below. Your name at birth creates your life. According to esoteric teachings, your soul chose your name at birth as well as the exact date, time and place of your birth. The energy vibration in the letters and numbers carry a code – the code of your life purpose, the map of your life (Ngan, 2013).

Astrology

It is written in the stars...

Carl Jung was fascinated with astrology because it tied in with his ideas about archetypes and the collective unconscious. He often drew up and studied his clients' natal charts to identify links to events in their lives. He felt that astrological data shed light on aspects of a person's personality that would otherwise have been challenging to understand (Snowden, 2006).

An astrological birth chart serves as a spiritual map of your life and can show your gifts and talents, as well as the challenges you face, and may help uncover your life purpose.

The sun shows where you shine:

♈ **Aries:** I am – energetic, driven, active, pioneering, dynamic, independent

♉ **Taurus:** I have – stable, persistent, domestic, practical, reliable

♊ **Gemini:** I think – versatile, dual, expressive, curious, quick-witted

♋ **Cancer:** I feel – intuitive, emotional, sensitive, sympathetic, domestic, devoted

♌ **Leo:** I will – confident, expressive, dramatic, ambitious, optimistic

♍ **Virgo:** I analyse – practical, scientific, meticulous, perfectionistic

♎ **Libra:** I balance – artistic, refined, diplomatic, sociable

♏ **Scorpio:** I desire – passionate, intense, penetrating, determined, investigative

♐ **Sagittarius:** I understand – philosophical, broad-minded, visionary, adventurous

♑ **Capricorn:** I use – ambitious, business-minded, practical, hard-working

♒ **Aquarius:** I know – humane, eccentric, friendly, loyal, original

♓ **Pisces:** I believe – compassionate, intuitive, introspective, sensitive

A natal chart shows the position of all the planets at the time of your birth. Astrology reveals the effect of these celestial bodies and their archetypal influences on you during your life.

The planets as archetypal energies

The term archetype has its origin in ancient Greek and refers to original or old type of patterns. The symbolism and images we find in stories and myths are what Jung called archetypes. They appear as recurring patterns of thinking and tend to be universal as they represent typical human experiences (Snowden, 2006). The associations made between planets, mythology and human characteristics are ancient. These associations are often universal and reflected in the mythology of antiquity (Parker, 1991).

- **Sun** – ego self, personality, main personal concerns, vitality

  The sun describes your sense of personal identity, your creative expression and your ability to realize your individual potential and gain recognition.

- **Moon** – emotions, instincts, habits

  The moon describes your emotional nature, your instinctual behaviour and unconscious response patterns and your sense of home and family.

- **Mercury** – communication, intellect, reason

  Mercury describes your manner of expression, your powers of communication and intellectual reasoning and your ability to formulate and articulate ideas and make decisions.

- **Venus** – love, beauty, art

  Venus describes your appreciation of beauty and the arts, your powers of attraction and your capacity for close personal relationships and love affairs.

- **Mars** – energy, action, desire, aggression

  Mars describes the way you act and assert yourself, your basic urges and desires, your drive and your fire and your ability to achieve personal goals.

- **Jupiter** – expansion, optimism, abundance

  Jupiter describes how you relate to the larger world beyond your personal self, how you expand in life and how you experience higher learning, travel, and religion.

- **Saturn** – the teacher; restriction, structure

  Saturn describes your experience of reality, your fears and inhibitions, what you are serious about and how you respond to society's rules. Saturn's actions are slow, restrictive, and lasting.

- **Uranus** – the awakener; rebellion, eccentricity, upheaval, revolution

  Uranus, a generational planet because it appears in the same sign for so many people, describes areas of personal and peer-group uniqueness, originality and eccentricity, your intuitive awareness and your ability to adapt to sudden change.

- **Neptune** – intuition, imagination, dreams

  Neptune, a generational planet, describes your personal and peer-group experience of spirituality and the mystical, and your powers of inspired imagination.

- **Pluto** – transformation

  Pluto, a generational planet, describes your personal and peer-group experience of upheavals, forces beyond individual control, power and irreversible changes. Pluto unearths the hidden.

- **Moon's north node** – your potential

  The moon's north node is a mathematical point – a point of expansion, potential and growth: your destination.

- **Moon's south node** – your karmic past

  The south node represents a set of talents and skills you've already mastered as well as habits and patterns that no longer profit you. It is your launching pad.

- **Chiron** – point of healing

  Chiron is a small outer planet, described as The Wounded Healer. Both a point of pain and a source of healing, Chiron shows where you have suffered and must find healing.

Numerology

Numerology is another esoteric tool as old as existence. Numbers are universal archetypal symbols. Pythagoras taught that numbers are the essence of all things. The letters of the alphabet all have numerical values, and all numbers can be reduced to nine cardinal numbers. These nine numbers not only symbolize specific archetypes, they also represent nine stages of development or growth cycle, much the same as in nature. First the seed goes into the soil – a new beginning. Nurturing brings the plant into growth. Eventually it flourishes, flowers and produces fruit to share. After the harvest it's time for completion and rest. The cycle ends and another begins.

A full numerology profile using names at birth and date of birth will reveal your gifts, talents, destiny, challenges, and lessons. Numerology is fairly simple. You can determine your life path number using your date of birth. Add up every digit in your date of birth until you have a single digit. For example, 28 July 1997 will be 2+8+7+1+9+9+7= 43 and 4+3=7. The life path number will be 7.

The following is a brief summary of the characteristics of the numbers 1 through 9 as elaborated by Milman (1993) and Decoz (*http://www.decoz.com/*).

1: **Leadership, Independence, Creativity and Confidence**

The number 1 represents the beginning, the source, the innovator, the originator, the pioneer, and the starter energy and uniqueness of the individual.

2: **Co-operation and Balance**

The 2 represents team-work, diplomacy and tact. It is a supportive number and people with the number 2 often play the role of advisor. They are caring, gentle and generous.

3: **Expression and Sensitivity**

The 3 is playful, creative, inspirational and motivating. Self-expression and communication are its central qualities. The emotional sensitivity of the 3 is a gift of refined intuition.

4: **Stability and Process**

The 4 is the foundation. People with a 4 are practical, sensible and have a sharp eye for details. They are orderly, systematic, methodical, precise, reliable and dependable. They do what they say they will do and are honest and trustworthy.

5: **Freedom and Discipline**

The 5 is dynamic and likes to experience adventure. The 5 is persuasive; a promoter and a salesperson par-excellence. People with a 5 are versatile and adaptable. They like to experiment and explore. Bright and quick-witted, they have a lust for life and can be easily lured into sensual pleasures and immediate gratification.

6: **Vision, Health, Healing and Family**

The 6 is about love, harmony and balance. They are home- and family-oriented, and community conscious. The 6 is the teacher and the healer. People with a 6 are idealistic, responsible, committed, sympathetic, protective, nurturing and self-sacrificial.

7: **Trust, Openness and Knowledge**

The 7 is the seeker of truth. Mentally strong, people with a 7 are analytical, focused, contemplative, and meditative. The 7 is the accumulator of knowledge and wisdom; the intellectual and abstract thinker. It is insightful and understanding, introspective and often withdrawn. The 7 is the scientist, philosopher, preacher, scholar, and sage.

8: **Power and Abundance**

The 8 is the chief-executive, leader and business person. Result-orientated, the 8 is powerful, ambitious, and money conscious, yet generous. People with an 8 are understanding, forgiving and broadminded. They understand money as a tool. The 8 represents the balance between the material and the spiritual world.

9: **Integrity and Wisdom**

The 9 is the humanitarian and the philanthropist. People with a 9 are self-sacrificial without the need for reward.

They are giving, sharing, loving, and caring. The 9 is the statesperson, politician, lawyer, writer, sage, philosopher and idealist. The 9 is here to serve and make the world a better place. Charismatic and inspirational, they motivate others through example.

Master Numbers

These are double-digit numbers such as 11, 22 and 33. Master numbers are the exception as they are not reduced to their digits. Double numbers intensify the digits. They are called Master numbers because they possess a higher-level power and potential than the other numbers.

Number 11

The Master Innovator or Master Illuminator. The 11 is highly intuitive, even psychic. Ideas and insight come to them intuitively. They are ideas generators and creative thinkers. They have a fine energy vibration and are emotionally sensitive.

Number 22

The Master Builder. The 22 is here to establish something practical of lasting significance for mankind, even on a global scale. It could be an actual building or an institute or a service. They are practical and grounded and highly gifted, able to conceive ideas and bring big goals into actual manifestation.

Number 33

The Master Teacher. A healer and helper to others, the 33 seeks to be of service to others. Often called the Spiritual Teacher, the 33 is sacrificial and has a strong spiritually empowering influence on others.

Earth is the soul's training ground. As such, we are often born into circumstances that allow us to experience the opposite of what we are to become. 'The soul learns through opposites. By exploring what you do not want, you get clear about what you want' (Schwartz, 2012). This may involve overcoming victimhood and finding self-empowerment. You may need to overcome feelings of shyness and unworthiness by growing into a great communicator and teacher. This learning and growth process enables us to heal and teach from the depths of our own experiences and wisdom. Karma is therefore your greatest gift. As you learn and overcome your karmic lessons, your gifts unfold and you are then able to step into your true purpose. Your purpose is often hidden where your fear lies. When we shy away from what we feel called to do out of fear, we create disease in the body. 'Once you claim your gifts of service, your life will begin to truly unfold' (Ngan 2013). These gifts of service are what you came to do and share in the world; your unique contribution. Your ultimate purpose is to be true to yourself, true to your chosen path and your true potential. Release anything that gets in the way of your expressing your true self.

The more you develop your intuitive ability – your ability to feel, know, trust, and surrender to your inner, higher guidance – the more gracefully and easily your life will flow.

Protection

As you begin to open up psychically, it's important to consider protecting yourself energetically – not from a basis of fear, because you are already safe, but to create sacred space, direct intention, and to keep your energy in a place of integrity.

Useful Methods of Self-protection:

Grounding:

Ground into your body and root into the earth so you start from a safe and firm foundation. To do this, close your eyes and breathe into the stomach. Then visualize yourself as a tree with roots spreading down into the earth.

Shielding:

Create a protective shield around your energy field to ward off unwanted entities and negative energy. To do this, visualize a glowing ball of light around you. Install an intention in it; for example: *Provide protection while radiating light, love, and joy.* Use your imagination to shape it into something symbolic to you, be it a rainbow or star or perhaps an element. Remember, fire is electric and expands outward. Water is magnetic and draws inward. Use shielding not to stop something from getting to you but to place yourself in the light and offer an area of high vibration around you to anyone you get in contact with. Your desire to give and love is what will stop all negative entities in their tracks.

Setting an intention:

Keep your energy directed and focused by setting a clear intention. Work with your guides and the archangels to keep you in the light.

Cutting and cleansing:

When your energy feels scattered, drained, or affected, or people you interacted with are still playing on your mind, cut, retract and cleanse the energy strands by using the Ho'oponopono meditation in Step 4.

Meditation to Meet with Your Guides

The following meditation is adapted from a meditation by Diane Steiner (1995).

This meditation is aimed to help you make conscious contact with your life guide and other guides.

Before you came to Earth to live this life, you made an agreement with your spirit guides regarding what this life was going to be about. Your spirit guides laid out all the opportunities and challenges that you could face during your lifetime, and together you agreed on what would happen. So, you agreed on your purpose and were given guides to assist you along the way. Some guides are with us throughout several lifetimes, and others are with us only for this one; and even in this lifetime, guides can come and go. Some guides come for a specific purpose and leave when it is fulfilled. Some remain in contact for a long time, others for a short period. Some may be departed loved ones.

Start by creating sacred space with candles and fragrances. Lie down on the floor with your knees bent so your feet make contact with the earth. Go through progressive relaxation, tightening and then relaxing muscle groups, starting from your feet and ending with your head. The body relaxed, bring your focus to your breathing, deepening the in-breath and making the out-breath twice as long.

Set your intention with the meditation: *I am ready to consciously meet my life guide.*

This meditation requires a deeper state of relaxation. I like to start by going through A Meditative Journey through the Chakras, as described in Appendix 2 – a journey through the colours of the rainbow towards ever-increasing finer vibrations of blues and purples that are naturally trance inducing; a journey that naturally progresses towards the deep purple of aether.

As you lie effortlessly on the floor, perfectly grounded in the body and connected to the earth, imagine your body getting gradually lighter. Your journey has taken you into the deep purple aether. If you can, visualize the deep purple aether becoming misty, or you might feel this happening as you experience a lightness, a floaty, drifty feeling, like rising into the mist. You can also chant the sound of aether: *IAO* (a drawn-out *eeeeee-aaaaaa-oooooo*). Eventually the mist begins to take shape as you begin to perceive the space where you want to meet your guide or guides. This space may create itself in your mind, or you can create it. It might be a beautiful room or a clearing in a magical forest.

Now invite your guide or guides to meet with you in this space. Some guides might not be easy to see. Not everyone can see or visualize the spirit beings. It is just as valid to inwardly hear the voice, to feel the presence of your spirit guide or smell a particular fragrance.

Pay close attention to everything you experience during this meditation.

- You may recognize your guide or guides or you may not. You may be meeting them again or for the first time.

- You can ask your guides to make themselves known. Ask for a name, who they are, what their purpose is in your life. If there are several guides present, ask them to come forward one at a time rather than all at once. It may take several meditations to familiarize yourself with your guides.

- You can have a discussion with your guides.

- You can ask for information – you might want to ask about your life purpose, the direction your life is taking, or for guidance and clarity.

- You may have specific questions about actions to take. Go ahead and ask. This is what your guides are here for.

- Your guides may have words of wisdom for you. The wisdom you receive may be very inspiring.

- Listen carefully, as if you are about to hear the most important thing you'll ever hear whispered to you.

- You guide may have a gift for you; a treasure. It could be a special ability, a source of wisdom, and as they offer this gift to you, you can accept it with gratitude.

- Treasure this gift and the wisdom you receive.

- Often guides have something they want to say to you – advice about your journey, your progress. Listen carefully. What is it you need to know at this point? Just take it in.

- Soon it will be time to go, so begin to thank your guides.

- Establish how you could meet again.

- Slowly bring your awareness back to the room as you begin to centre yourself and your vision becomes more focused. Open your eyes and re-energize by stretching and taking a few deep breaths.

- Ground back into the body.

- Make some notes of your experience in a journal while it is fresh in your mind.

Visit _http://liftingtheveilsofillusion.co.uk/meditations/_ to download a free audio meditation: Meditation to connect with your inner guidance.

Journey through the Chakras: Sixth Chakra Contemplation and Visualization

Chakra	Sixth chakra: the third-eye chakra, between the eyebrows
Function	Inner vision, intuition, wisdom, psychic perception
Emotion	Fear-related limiting beliefs
Colour	Indigo
Spiritual Law	Seek only the truth
Meditation	I see
Element	Light
Crystal	Lapis lazuli, sodalite

The third-eye chakra is located between the eyebrows. Its colour is indigo – dark blue – and its element is light. This is the centre of your psychic perception. It promotes inner vision and intuition, concentration and insight. You may want to promote your inner vision now by letting the eyes roll up to this area between the brows and noticing the inner light there within the pineal gland. It helps to darken the room at first. Start by rolling your eyes upwards and to the right, then upwards and to the left. Then, roll your eyes straight up as if you want to look at the light in the pineal gland. You can meditate on this light, which is spirit in you. You may perceive the light more as swirling colours or spots of light, and that is fine. And as you meditate on the light ask for inner vision, to be able to perceive the truth, to see the world as it really is – all energy and pure potentiality.

Purpose

Your purpose is not worked out
Like a mathematical algorithm;
It is not a product of reason.

It is a product of love.

And like time through nature's seasons
Or light through a crystal prism
What is within will change without.

BY ANDREA NOLAN
ONTOLOGICAL LEADERSHIP COACH AND INSPIRATIONAL POET

Step 7: Living In the Present Moment

Illusion 7	Time IS an illusion
	Past and future IS an illusion that causes stress and keeps me in the ego
	Ego IS illusion
Reality	Everything happens now
	You are divine
Shift	Become and live as your higher self
	Recognize that there is no right and wrong
Transformational Meditation	Come back to now
	Come back to your true self: connect with your higher self
	Draw down the light

Your Three Minds

The more you make peace with the past, heal relationships, and release emotions and limiting beliefs, the more quickly you can access the higher planes of existence. The more you come into the peace and creativity of the present moment, the more you *are* your higher self.

Step 3 touched on the three minds from a creation perspective. Step 7 expands on the nature and functions of the higher mind and the evolutionary process of becoming your higher self and living as your higher self.

YOUR HIGHER CONSCIOUSNESS

- Is your guardian spirit; divine in you; creator of your universe
- Is the real you that travels beyond time and space and has always existed
- Is your connection to the higher realms
- Is your source of intuition and inspiration
- Is the perfect you
- Is who you are becoming
- Is your sixth sense
- Is love, joy, peace, fearlessness
- Is all-powerful and humble
- Has no personal investment or attachments
- Sees you and everyone else as perfect
- Will always give you what you ask for
- Can create anything you ask
- Can uncreate anything you don't want; e.g., disease, unhappiness
- Is the source of manifestation
- Has the blueprint of perfect health
- Is beyond judgement; all-forgiving
- Respects free will and must be asked

YOUR CONSCIOUS MIND

- Decides
- Focuses
- Concentrates
- Clarifies
- Specifies
- Directs your unconscious mind

YOUR UNCONSCIOUS MIND

- Runs your body
- Stores memory
- Generates, stores and distributes energy
- Is the domain of emotions
- Maintains instincts and habits
- Controls and maintains perceptions and beliefs
- Is symbolic – uses and responds to symbols (e.g., dreams, imagination, visualizations)
- Is highly suggestible and picks up on every thought – use only positive language
- Follows orders and wants to please you – specify exactly what you want
- Is creative; magical
- Is the key/path to your higher self

The ultimate goal is wholeness: the merging of the three minds into one. When you manifest your desired outcomes with one mind, then what you want, wants you. What you bring about will align with your life purpose. It will be for your highest good and for the greater good and will therefore manifest itself much more quickly.

Nature and Functions of Your Higher Consciousness

Your higher consciousness, also called your higher self or guardian spirit, is the divine in you; your connection to the higher realms. Your higher self is the eternal you that has always existed; the real you that goes beyond time and space; beyond past and future. Your higher self is beyond gender – balanced male and female energy.

Connecting and communicating with your higher self can make everything right for you. Your higher self has the ability to recognize causes, the sources of events, and this ability is a key factor in healing. Your higher self has the power to know, predict and effect the future. Your future is not cast in stone – there are multiple potential outcomes. You always have free will. Your higher self has knowledge of your life purpose and can guide you on your path. Your higher self has insight into the entire universe and is the source of your intuition and inspiration.

Extrasensory perception is a function of your higher mind; your higher self has the power to produce gifts such as clairvoyance, clairaudience, inner knowing, intuition and the ability to communicate telepathically and heal distantly.

Your higher self sees you as perfect, sees everyone else as perfect and sees your life in perfect order. Being the perfect you, your higher self never makes mistakes. When you operate as your higher self, you do so free of mistakes. Your higher self is beyond judgement and all-forgiving because it sees all as one. Your higher self is beyond description, beyond language – it can only be experienced.

Your higher self is the source of manifestation. It has the blueprint of perfect health, so approaching your higher self can bring about instant healing. It has the power to remove (uncreate) anything that serves you no longer, such as physical and psychological disease, complexes, emotions, fixations and false identification, and can do so instantaneously (Freedom Long, 1953).

Your higher self respects the conscious mind's free will and therefore must be asked for assistance. It wants you to have peace and always gives you what you ask for.

In the process of evolution, the higher self represents who you are becoming.

Connecting with Your Higher Self

The higher the level of your energy vibration (as illustrated in the ladder of emotional levels, Step 2), the closer you are to your higher self. To foster a close connection with it, your higher self wants you to be free from past negative emotions, limiting beliefs, false identifications and energy-draining connections.

Your unconscious mind holds the key to connection with your higher self. We can't consciously conceive of the higher self. Communication is channelled through your unconscious mind in symbolic language, visualization, feelings, sensations in the body, gut feelings and the like.

The Path of Personal Evolution

The path of growth and development through the seven chakras to higher levels of awareness is also a path of growth from physical to emotional and then mental and finally spiritual. The path takes us from dependence to independence and eventually interdependence.

Jung says that like the (true higher) self, we have the unconscious mind from birth, out of which the conscious mind emerges in the course of childhood development. Developing a strong and effective ego helps us function in the outer world. To develop a healthy ego, we must bring more and more of our unconscious habits and patterns into conscious awareness. Eventually we reach a stage when we realize that our true higher self is more real and more important than the ego. At this stage, we begin integrating the minds into one, and eventually we may begin to attain higher consciousness (Snowden, 2006).

To know who you are becoming, you must familiarize yourself with the qualities of your higher self. This is a paradox, however, as you are already who you are becoming. It is more a homecoming to yourself; a fulfilment of who you truly are. To further your personal evolution, begin to operate more from the level of your higher self. This work will expose the illusion of the ego further. We don't fight the ego – rather, we integrate it. You only have to recognize the ego and then have the intention to surrender it to the higher self. The higher self embraces the ego and brings it in, into oneness – a powerful visualization that can be incorporated into a meditation.

Integrating the minds into one brings us into wholeness. The word *whole* is the root and true meaning of words such as *health, holy, holistic* and *healing*.

When we achieve this wholeness, and we know we are all one, the ego judgements, projections and reactions stop. When you realize that what you react to in others is also in you, the ego is exposed and you stop seeing yourself as a victim (Tolle, 2005). Instead of projecting, you are now free to extend yourself, your true light, your service in this world.

The Essence of Enlightenment

When you shift your consciousness into your higher self and operate as your higher self,

- You are truly fearless

- You feel unconditional love for all things and everyone

- You have access to true wisdom – all-knowing, all-seeing

- You are all-powerful yet humble – something the ego is incapable of

- You are all-forgiving, all-accepting

- You are beyond judgement, beyond the duality of right and wrong, good and bad; everything is just an experience

- You are free from attachments to outcomes and personal investments

- You are mindful, flowing in the moment

- You experience peace, joy and bliss

- Your life is more about *being* than *doing*

- You are of one mind – integrated, whole and aligned

- Instant healing is possible

- Instant manifestation is achievable

- You can control your thoughts and communicate telepathically

- You don't fix things (nothing is damaged), you just create another reality – of perfection.

'The decision to make the present moment
into your friend, is the end of the ego.
Time is what the ego feeds on'.
– ECKHART TOLLE

Path of Evolution

EGO World of Form and Particles	HIGHER SELF World of Energy and Waves
Head	Heart
Fear	Love; unconditional love; fearlessness
Stress	
Judgement; blame	Calm; expanded awareness
	Forgiveness; compassion
Limitations	Infinite potential; creativity; energy
Hostile universe	Friendly universe, of which you are a much-loved child
Separateness	
Selfishness	Interconnectedness; oneness
Scarcity	Kindness
Control	Universal abundance
Sadness/depression	Peace
Anxiety; fear of the unknown	Joy
	Acceptance; trust; sense of adventure
Limiting beliefs	Empowering beliefs
Knowledge	
Addictions	Intuitive knowing; inspiration; sixth sense
Anger; frustration	Freedom
Guilt	Patience
	Self-love; forgiveness
Disease	Perfect health
Living in the past and future	Being in the moment, in the flow
Never enough time	Expanded time; expanded NOW
Doing	Being
Life seems difficult; problems	Life seems effortless; solutions
Projecting perceptions	Extending; expressing self
Resistance	Non-resistance; embracing
Happiness comes from outside	Joy comes from inside
Arrogance; force	Humility; all-powerful
Duality of right, wrong; good, bad	Balance; beyond duality, everything just is
Attachments; personal investments	Free from attachments to outcomes and personal investments

The Power of Love

To become your higher self and attain the abilities of the higher mind, you must step into a higher power. It is essential that we embrace this higher power, which is quite unlike ego, arrogance and force. Only the higher self can be all-powerful and humble at the same time. Many of us on the spiritual path feel challenged by the idea of power, but you can't use your power until you own it.

As Marianne Williamson reminds us in *A Return to Love* (1992):

Our deepest fear is not that we are inadequate.
Our deepest fear is that we are powerful beyond measure.
It is our light, not our darkness, that most frightens us.

How do you step into this higher power? Ultimately, divine power is love. We must evolve out of fear into love; the love that is the essence of life, the love that is the essence of us all. That which we seek is that which we are. We are becoming who we already are. This is self-realization. To really know who we are we must journey home to love, and reaching it requires opening our hearts and walking with awareness.

The destination is common to us all, yet we each have our own path to tread. Home is not necessarily a place – it is a state of consciousness. It is the inner knowing, gained through personal experience, that our true nature is love, joy and peace. To become aware of this, we must identify and dismantle the ego's illusions, for it is our outdated attachment to the illusionary world of the ego that prevents us from experiencing a life that is truly peaceful, loving and magical.

> **'We are connected to the source of the universe in the very moment of now'.**
> **- DEEPAK CHOPRA**

Your true higher self transcends all duality and unites everything into one. As we become of one (higher) mind, we become one with everything and everyone in a whole new way. This path is the only true reality, and it exists in its entirety in the present moment.

Meditation: Connecting with Your Higher Self

Relax, become aware of your breathing. Deepen the in-breath and make the out-breath twice as long – 1-to-2-ratio breathing. A longer out-breath activates the parasympathetic nervous system, telling the body it's time to relax.

Take note of what is going on in the mind, just noticing.

Begin to still the mind using the breath. Breathe out all the business; let it go.

Let the world and its issues fade away as you go inside.

Become aware of your body. Spend a moment in gratitude for the body – all its automatic processes keeping you energized and healthy, naturally.

Relax the body.

Become aware of your feelings, your emotions. How are you feeling today? Not judging in any way, just taking note.

Now shift beyond these feelings.

Who are you beyond the body?
Who are you beyond the emotions?

Shift your awareness into the heart. It may help to place the palm of one hand on your heart. If it's not easy to switch the mind off, begin to hum (*hmmmmmm*) into the heart, or sound a drawn-out *aaaaaa* that opens your heart centre.

Take your consciousness, your attention, into the heart. Breathe into the heart, 1-to-2-ratio breathing. Hear and feel your heartbeat. Begin to relax the heart area, feel it becoming warm as you open the heart centre. Spread that warmth throughout the body.

Your heart is the centre of your intuition, where your inspiration and ideas come from when you are relaxed. Your imagination opens up and you can be infinitely creative. Your heart is the centre of love, joy and peace. Spend a few moments in love, appreciation and gratitude for who you are. You are totally unique and immensely valuable. Your life has a special purpose – one that only you can fulfil.

Settle in the present moment, in the heart.

Say to yourself:

My body is relaxed,

My heart is at peace,

My mind is calm,

My mind is in the service of my heart,

I am at peace,

All is well.

(Drop your hand and let it relax in your lap)
Feel a sense of space and expansion here at the heart.
Allow your awareness to expand beyond yourself.

Wider and wider. Take the whole room (or wherever you are) into your awareness. Expand your awareness beyond the room, beyond the town where you are, beyond your country, beyond the Earth, beyond the planets, beyond the solar system, beyond the galaxy, into the wider universe. Take it all into your awareness. Notice it's just one thing, with which you are one.

Enter a state of oneness with everything and everyone – a state of unity of consciousness.

Enter the light, the void, the field where everything is just a wave of potential: the fifth dimension.

Here at the heart you are connected to the source of life, your source of energy and good health.

Here you are your higher self. You are a being of light: feel it, connect to it. You are the light; you are pure energy.

Your essential nature is love, joy, peace and bliss.

As your higher self you have access to infinite wisdom and infinite potential. You are safe and you can trust who you are becoming.

Free from the past, out of the future – free from fear, free to live fearlessly.

As your higher self all your longings, desires and needs are gone.

Here you have everything you need already; you are complete.

You have access to abundant resources, already inside you. You are an all-powerful creator.

Become aware of and connect to your higher self; your true self; the self that has always existed. This is you in your perfect state.

Your higher self is the presence of the universal intelligence within you; it is the creator of your universe, the source of your guidance and inspiration.

As your higher self it's natural to love unconditionally.

Your higher self is all-accepting, all-knowing, all-forgiving, beyond judgement; it sees you and your life as perfect.

Your higher self is the source of magic and miracles, prosperity, happiness and good health.

Being in your higher self unleashes your full potential.

Being in your higher self gives you peace and gives you access to the higher abilities of the mind and spirit.

Rest and abide as your higher self.

In a moment, when you bring yourself back, do so with the intention to stay in your higher self and live from this level of your higher self – magically, powerfully.

Ground this light of high vibration back into the body.

Visit *http://liftingtheveilsofillusion.co.uk/meditations/* to download a free audio meditation: Meditation to connect with your higher self.

Journey through the Chakras: Seventh Chakra Contemplation and Visualization

Chakra	Seventh chakra: the crown chakra, just above the head
Function	Higher consciousness, spiritual intelligence, enlightenment, bliss, transcendence, awareness
Emotion	Love, Joy, Peace
Colour	Purple
Spiritual Law	Live in the present moment
Meditation	I am
Element	Thought
Crystal	Amethyst, clear quartz, selenite

The crown chakra is located just above your head. This centre energizes the upper brain. It promotes positive thought patterns, inspiration and imagination. This chakra relates to spiritual well-being and connects us with our higher self and the higher realms. Constantly channelling life-force energy into our system, it aligns and balances all our chakras. Visualize a beautiful purple colour emanating from the crown at the top of your head. Draw down the light into the body. Now visualize all seven chakras perfectly aligned and balanced.

A Journey Completed

You have undertaken and completed a significant transformational journey of personal evolution. You have invested intent, time and effort in your own growth and persevered through all the key steps. Congratulations! You can rightly celebrate the person you have become as a result.

You may want to pause and reflect at this point:

How have my perceptions changed?

What new insights have I gained?

How have I changed as a person?

Do I feel more peaceful now, with the old reactive ego integrated into the whole?

How have my relationships changed?

What new possibilities are opening up to me as I climb the ladder from negative to positive emotions and to higher levels of consciousness?

How has my external world changed as I reflect a new version of myself out into the world?

You may not be aware of the extent of the change at first. People around you may see more light in you now, in the same way Jenny's friends did. That brings us back to Carole, Jenny and Joe, whom we met in the introduction.

Carole has since moved on from the children's charity, where she gained invaluable experience. She set up her own events organization company, which specializes in events for young people. She thoroughly enjoys her new freedom and independence and the vibrant energy of the young people she works with. Her relationship is happy and solid now, and her health and energy returned seemingly by itself.

Jenny decided to live the dream and travel extensively while teaching all over the world. Determined to make the most of life, she explored beautiful places and met wonderful people. This afforded her opportunities to attend unique workshops and courses that helped her explore and deepen her spiritual interests. She finally met a man who has real appreciation for the person she is. Together they set up a feng-shui-based interior design business and enjoy creating harmonious and healthy domestic and work spaces.

Joe started a thriving marketing business that employs a number of gifted creative people. After it was all running smoothly, he started studying psychology with the view of applying it to progressive, personalized marketing. He's a happy bachelor for now. He'd rather take his time and meet the right person when the time is right.

Whatever the nature of your journey, turbulent or smooth, your experiences may take on new meaning now that the old victim mindset is exposed. You know now you are the powerful creator of your own life and have infinite choice. You can now just observe the old reactive, suffering-creating ego as it plays out the last of its programming while lovingly correcting it, reminding it there is another way – a way of love and positive experiences. As you continue to release any old resistance and force, you are increasingly free to flow with your intuitive, heart-based inner guidance. With the old fears gone, a whole new realm of possibilities opens up to you. You are free now to explore your highest potential and open up to the true purpose of your life – being your true magnificent self here on an unfolding, glorious new Earth.

A Reflection on A Course In Miracles

'Nothing real can be threatened.
Nothing unreal exists.
Herein lies the peace of God'.
– A COURSE IN MIRACLES

When I was asked to write a short piece about my experience of A Course In Miracles, I spent some time imagining that my writing might contain something inspiring, even creative, that would perhaps *impress* you, the reader, with my understanding of spiritual matters! I further went on to imagine the positive feedback I might get... uh-oh! All thoughts of the ego! The underlying purpose being for **ME** to *impress* **YOU** – and thus emphasizing the ego thoughts of **separation** between us. Then, inevitably, I started to be concerned that I might indeed **fail** to *impress*. I became preoccupied about what

I should write about: How am I ever going to condense the philosophy of the Course In Miracles into a few short paragraphs and do the course justice? The responsibility was starting to weigh heavier! My mind was beginning to spin with all the negative thoughts starting to pile up. I was feeling **GUILT** even before I had put pen to paper! Then came **FEAR** of criticism – what if you didn't like what I wrote? – and **FEAR** of not being good enough: more thoughts of the ego again! Ego thoughts of failing, overwhelming responsibility, guilt and fear reveal the **ego's distorted beliefs of separation** between us. These feelings of fear and guilt then **block** the awareness of love's presence.

All thoughts of conflict are of the ego. And it's so easily done, to slide into ego. Before you know it there's that familiar feeling of restriction; demanding and commanding. **Of becoming that small, separated self.**

Be still. There is an inner voice. This quiet voice, my one self/holy spirit is my trusted guide out of this maze, when there is conflict.

Before writing this piece I was led to consider **Lesson 178 in ACIM '…I am but Love'.** My one self reminds me of this truth. In a holy instant can come a complete change in thinking, and that is the miracle. Awareness can be brought back from the ego's beliefs in fear and guilt based on separation and lack to the realization that separation never existed.

As I ask myself what is my intention in writing this piece, I am brought back to my purpose and my function. From the course comes this wonderful dedication: 'I am here only to be truly helpful, I am here to represent him who sent me. I do not need to worry therefore what to say or what to do because he who sent me will direct me. I am content to be wherever he wishes, knowing that he goes there with me. And I will be healed as I let him teach me to heal'.

So I step back from the angst of my ego and ask myself: What is my intention, my purpose, my function, in writing this piece? That quiet voice reminds me to remember that every choice I make is a choice for love and right-minded thinking. A choice for peace.

And there ends all ego-based conflict. My purpose is to remember that I am but love and there is no separation. That is my purpose and function in writing these words.

Love Is All. And **All Is ONE.** Just as **ego is separation.** Fear and guilt are simply reflections of ego's distorted belief in separation – until in that holy instant of remembering, all fears and guilt are released and forgiven. A remembrance that **Love is All.** In a holy instant all distorted ego-based beliefs of guilt and fear separation and lack are healed. True perception replaces distorted thinking with peace and joy. A knowing that there is no separation. Love is all. '**...I am but love**'.

How simple life then becomes, without the conflict of the ego. Every choice is a choice for peace, and true perception brings peace. My intention, my purpose and function, is the extension of peace, and the extension of love. *These are the gifts I am entrusted with.* Love is all **includes YOU AND ME.** All Is One. Rejoice: there is no separation, only love. Blessings to you,

BY ANNE CALDWELL
MENTAL HEALTH PROFESSIONAL

Brink

There will come a time
When the only door that will open for you
Is the one through which you must walk.

Do not be afraid.
Your future beckons and Destiny awaits.

There is a light shining beyond
Where the gifts you have been given
Will be received with open arms.

Let down your guard
For I am your companion now.

BY ANDREA NOLAN
ONTOLOGICAL LEADERSHIP COACH AND INSPIRATIONAL POET

Epilogue: Entering a New Era of Enlightenment

We live in a pivotal time in human evolution. We have the privilege to be here on Earth during a shift out of the 2000-year-long Age of Pisces into the Age of Aquarius. In fact, we are here to usher in the new era by being the change. The outgoing values of materialism, competitiveness, exploitation, war and conflict are making way for peace, kindness, compassion, sharing and caring on a grand scale. We are already experiencing this change, as all over the world, light workers (see Appendix 4) of many kinds are taking initiatives to care for the environment, support people in challenging situations and develop new inventions. Although there has been a move towards spirituality for a while, there is now evidence of a mass awakening to ourselves as spiritual beings.

Our ancestors predicted this time of mass awakening. Prophesies of the ancient rishis, Mayans, Maori, Aborigines, Buddhists and Jews pointed to this time – the time when one age would end and another would begin. A time of radical change; a time of mass awakening from spiritual amnesia; a time of recovered memory – of remembering who we truly are and what we are capable of.

They also predicted this spiritual amnesia, materialism, exploitation of Earth and its natural resources; they predicted our imbalances and our fall into density. They said that we are the generation living in this time of the shift and that the change is up to us. We are not to be passive observers, wondering what will happen. It is up to us to create the kind of world we want to live in. Our choices will determine the outcome and the quality of life that we take with us into the new era.

A theme runs in their prophecies: 'return to the ancient wisdom'. The ancient teachings – that all is energy, that we are all connected and that we are divine – will spring up everywhere again, like a groundswell. Quantum scientists have assisted greatly; new understandings of energy confirm the ancient wisdom. Firstly, the prophesies predicted a return to nature – to simple, sustainable living and the observing of the cycles of nature and the planets. Secondly, they predicted a return to unity – living as one, in love and support of one another. Thirdly, they predicted a return to the light. This involves a process of purification and raising energy vibrations that will ultimately result in a change of form. As we choose the light and embody more light, we come out of our current density of form and gradually become light beings again. As we become lighter, we are able to fully integrate our higher consciousness, the higher self, into the body and live as fifth-dimensional beings here on Earth.

A critical mass may well be achieved in our lifetime; a critical mass of people acting from a place of love, compassion, kindness and peace. This will tip humanity into a new era of peace; a new existence of enlightenment.

The ancient Mayans observed the cycles of the planets and the stars, and their prophecies came about through in-depth studies of these grand cosmic cycles. They observed the precession of the equinoxes. Carl Jung was interested in this precession and also believed that this phenomenon has far-reaching effects upon both historic events and human spirituality. 'Each 2000-year change heralds the beginning of a new spiritual trend' (Snowden, 2006). These changes can be tracked back in history.

We have chosen to be here at this time for our own evolution and to assist with healing family and group karma. Carl Jung referred to the fact that many of our personal psychological problems arise from family or cultural karma – problems our forebears leave unresolved are passed on to be sorted out by the next generation. 'He said that many problems are more to do with the social environment than the individual and are therefore linked to the collective unconscious' (Snowden, 2006).

As a light worker you may feel challenged by this task: *There is so much to do out there. Where do I start?* We don't effect change just by working 'out there'. It is through inner work that we bring about change in the outer world. The inside creates the outside. Our work is always an inside job. We are all connected. As you change, the world around you changes.

As Marianne Williamson (1992) observed: 'We're an interesting generation, we just don't see that about ourselves. When I first realised what a decisive time this is, that the decisions made on this planet in the next 20 years will determine whether or not mankind survives much longer, I was afraid for the world. The fate of the world is left up to us? Not us, I thought. Anyone but us. We're spoilt brats, morally bankrupt. But when I looked closely, what I saw surprised me. We're not bad, we're wounded. And our wounds are simply our opportunities to heal'.

Our generation is indeed the generation living in a turning point in history; in human evolution. To make it through, to usher in a new era of unity consciousness, we are to overcome fear and any perceived limitations – for good. The ego cannot come through with us, as it represents fear and duality. To enter an era of unity, love and light, which we are doing right now, we are healing and releasing all karma and finally ending the wheel of karma. Karma served its purpose. We've been learning through experiencing opposites; we developed beliefs such as 'no pain no gain'. The time of suffering can indeed be over now. The energy is right for it. Robert Schwartz (2012) describes the new human: 'The new human will move beyond the learning-through-suffering paradigm. Less driven by fear, we will find that curiosity, creativity and love become our primary motivation to grow and learn'.

The ego is attached to suffering. It has been running a programme of suffering for so long, it doesn't know another way. We have to watch this ingrained programme and as we integrate the ego, reassure it that there is another way; a way of joy and love. We may have to remind ourselves of this until learning through positive, joyful experiences becomes our effortless new habit.

'In effortless being the Universe
self-organises and evolves.
So do we.'
– DEEPAK CHOPRA

This may well be the last lifetime for rebalancing, and so a lot is being crammed in. Chris Thomas, in *The Journey Home* (1998), describes how this ending of the process of karma means that we are finally able to begin the process of consciousness integration; of integrating the higher self fully into the physical body.

A door is finally closing on the past. History has served its purpose. The time has arrived to forget previously accepted patterns of judgement and fear-based thought. Now we've turned a page and have a blank sheet, a new beginning. It's time to forge a new future, a new age, a new Earth inside each one of us.

Eckhart Tolle (2005) describes the dawning of the new Earth: 'We are in the midst of a momentous event in the evolution of consciousness, but they won't be talking about it in the news tonight. On our planet, and perhaps simultaneously in many parts of our galaxy and beyond, consciousness is awakening from the dream of form'.

It is important to know that change doesn't come through fighting the old systems that seem wrong in the world. Fighting systems unnecessarily drains energy and simply energizes the very things we don't want. Outdated systems of self-interest, autocracy and material gain will cause their own demise. We have been seeing that happening all over the world.

Instead of fighting the existing system, rather create a new reality. As with all things, create it in your mind first. Ask yourself: What kind of world do I want to live in? Meditate on it, visualize it and usher it in through your thoughts and your actions; by living a fifth-dimensional life as your higher self.

This is the greatest time to be alive on Earth, and we have unprecedented opportunity for spiritual advancement and enlightenment. We are receiving great assistance from the unseen world. As predicted by the ancients, a rare and unique cosmic alignment of the Earth, the planets and our sun with the centre of the galaxy, the Milky Way, means high-frequency light is reaching us unhindered – a light that informs us and transforms us.

This shift from one era into another brings a radical change in consciousness, a shift in our understanding. We will see things differently. As the new age unfolds, we are shifting to a new values level.

OUTGOING VALUES:	NEW AGE VALUES:
Pisces (past 2000 years)	**Aquarius (coming 2000 years)**
• Materialism	• Spirituality; letting go of ego
• Competition	• Sharing; cooperation; generosity;
• Success	• Nurturing; support; goodwill
• Exploitation	• Sustainability; respect for natural resources
• Scarcity	• Self-sufficiency; return to simple living; minimalism
• Separateness	
• Individualism	• Respect for Earth, everyone and everything
• Differences and imbalances:	• Interconnectedness; oneness; community
- Nations	
- Cultures	• Equality; fairness; integrity;
- Borders	• Respect for all; common good, global community; balanced male and female energy
- Religions	
- Gender	
• Secrecy	• Openness; honesty; transparency (living as if people can read your thoughts)
• War; conflict	
• Technology; science	• Peace; joy; harmony; compassion
• Fear-based	• Creativity; flexibility
• Dominance	• Unconditional love
• Autocracy	• Empowerment of all
• Fast-paced life	• Slow-paced life; youth; health

Fifth-dimensional Living on a New Earth

On an individual level, the transition from third- to fifth-dimension being is a leap in evolution. It requires restructuring belief systems and energies and raising the vibration of the physical and subtle bodies. It requires transcending ego and negative thoughts and feelings. It requires personal healing. When you live more and more as a fifth-dimensional being, so much more becomes available to enjoy and explore.

On a communal level perhaps we will find new ways of living in close connection with the environment, in self-sustained, cooperative communities. Perhaps we will invent healthier construction technology, new means of travel, alternative energy sources, and a form of exchange, monetary or otherwise, much more viable than our current crumbling monetary system. The newly transformed Earth may well be a place of joy, peace, harmony and compassion beyond imagination – a place of generosity, trust, openness and positive support for everyone. As fifth-dimensional beings we will be energetically transformed, have higher psychic attainments and be motivated to serve, support and care for all, joyfully. Living in unity, we will do only what is for the highest good of everyone and the planet. We will care for the Earth and be as one, interconnected whole, responding to the needs of others. Free from ego and judgement. Free from any power struggle and personal agenda. Rather than working purely for financial survival out of fear and insecurity, we will do the work that satisfies our souls. People will be motivated by love, creative expression, the desire to help and serve. The old lack mindset gone, we will experience true abundance. Thought will manifest instantly and we will have everything we need. Happy to share everything, we may not necessarily have to possess and own things such as cars. Our hearts will be open. We will enjoy recovered youth and health as our natural state.

> *'As more of humanity practice heart-based living,*
> *it will qualify the "rite of passage" into*
> *the next level of consciousness,*
> *using our heart's intuitive guidance'.*
> **– DOC CHILDRE**

Perhaps, as the ancients predicted, we will move beyond time and beyond our dependency on technology. As we open up to the abilities of the higher mind, we will use our minds to do the things we rely on our gadgets to do for us now. We will sense others' needs intuitively and communicate telepathically. To do this, our minds will need to be unguarded, open and transparent. How pure will we have to be to have transparent minds, happy for others to pick up on our every thought? This is a mere glimpse of the new Heaven on Earth.

The Journey Continues

'What next?' you may ask. The journey is ongoing. There is always more to learn and discover. Enjoy the journey. From time to time you may desire a helpful nudge to your next level of evolution. Stay in touch. Visit _www.brightfuturenow.co.uk_ and join our signature soul-coaching programme – in person or online, wherever you are in the world. Also, sign up to _www.liftingtheveilsofillusion.co.uk_ to enjoy ongoing access to the audio meditations and keep up to date with the latest developments, products, courses, workshops and talks. Seeing you all at these events and hearing your stories is always a delight.

Appendix 1

Lifting the 7 Veils of Illusion: 7 Steps towards Spiritual Enlightenment

Illusion 1	I live in a world of circumstances I am a victim of random circumstances I am affected by people and circumstances
Reality	You live in a world of experience created through your own thinking Your choices and thoughts create your outcomes Thoughts create emotions with vibrations that attract likeness to you You perceive the world not as it is, but as you are You can only achieve what you believe you can Any perceived limitation is self-imposed All your experiences are on the inside; they only appear to be on the outside The inner creates the outer
Shift	Make essential mental shifts from effect to cause; victim to creator Take full responsibility for everything happening in your life Become the co-creator of your life Take 100 percent responsibility because it is 100 percent empowering
Mindfulness Meditation	Reflect mindfully on thoughts, beliefs and perceptions

Illusion 2	The world is a dangerous place Fear IS the illusion
Reality	Fear exists only in the mind Fear is contractive and limiting You are always safe Love is all there is When the fear goes, you can access love and positivity and open up to your true potential
Shift	Honour emotions as messages Learn, and let go of all fear
Healing Meditation	Heal and release negative emotions

Illusion 3	Only what I can see and touch is real I have only this conscious mind
Reality	You are a multidimensional being moving between dimensions to create your reality You have three minds and four bodies
Shift	Open up to the unseen magical realm Become a magical creator of your life
Manifestation Meditation	Create, communicate Set intention, ask

Illusion 4	We are separate
Reality	We are all one - interconnected
Shift	Practise unconditional love, compassion and forgiveness *Remember:* What I do to others, I do to myself What I think of others, I think of myself I see in others who I am
Healing Meditation	Heal relationships, forgive, reconnect

Illusion 5	Only humans have consciousness
Reality	Everything is interconnected We are all one with nature, made of the same elements - the web of life Consciousness is in everything: the planet, plants, animals Through connection and balance you create your own health
Shift	Return to nature; live in harmony with its cycles
Ritual Meditation	Honour the elements and natural cycles

Illusion 6	I am alone; I am lost; I have no purpose I am faced with random events
Reality	You are divinely guided, moment by moment Your higher self knows your chosen purpose (which you are here to discover)
Shift	Flow with life Align your intentions with your higher mind Create with one mind, for your highest good Follow your intuition
Intuitive Meditation	Communicate, ask Connect with inner guidance

Illusion 7	Time IS an illusion Past and future IS an illusion that causes stress and keeps me in the ego Ego IS illusion
Reality	Everything happens now You are divine
Shift	Become and live as your higher self Recognize that there is no right and wrong
Transformational Meditation	Come back to now Come back to your true self: connect with your higher self Draw down the light

Appendix 2

The Seven Chakras: Our Path of Growth and Development

So much has been written about the body's energy centres – the chakras. The following is not a definitive description of the chakras; rather, it's a wonderful journey through them to illustrate our path of growth and evolution in life.

We know now the universe is made of energy. This cosmic energy connects with our bodies through the chakras. They are not part of the physical body but part of the subtle energy body. The concept of the chakras has its roots in the Indian yogic system and can be traced back to many other ancient traditions.

The seven chakras reflect a path of growth and evolution from physical development (survival and tribal), to emotional development (creative expression), intellectual development and intuitive perception through to spiritual evolution. It is a beautiful path of self-discovery, and the chakras are profoundly important in regards to our health and well-being. The energy system is the mind-body link.

When we learn how to work with the chakras, we can balance and energize our bodies. The chakras are often worked with in therapy sessions because when we develop a problem, we literally develop a block in our energy system. So therapy and healing is aimed at unblocking energy, at opening up the energy centres of the body so that energy can flow freely through the system. This keeps us balanced and healthy. The chakra colours mirror those of the rainbow and take us from dense colours and lower dimensions to finer vibrations of colour and higher dimensions.

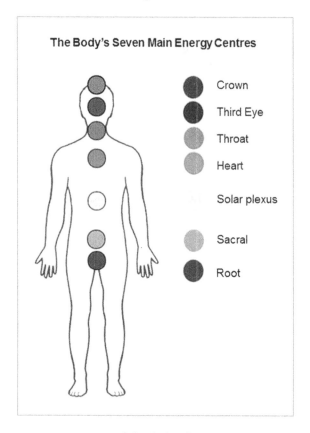

'The chakras'

The first energy centre: the root chakra
Survival

The base, or root, chakra is about stability, security, safety and physical survival. This chakra is connected to our legs and feet, through which we connect to the earth's energy and ground ourselves. Here at the root we are faced with physical needs related to the body, our physical environment and our connection to the Earth. The base chakra is red, and when it is healthy, open and flowing, we enjoy good physical health.

Our most basic lessons in life revolve around satisfying our physical needs, such as safety, nourishment, vitality and health. At this beginning stage of our lives we are dependent on others for surviving in this world. Later, we are to take charge of our own safety and security. Here at the root, the foundation is laid for our path of growth and development in life.

The second energy centre: the sacral chakra
Tribal

The sacral chakra is named after the sacrum – the back of the pelvis. The name implies it is a sacred place. The energy here is divine; this is the centre of procreation and creativity; the life force. This is also the centre of our emotions. The word emotion implies movement. Here we find fluidity and movement. It is feminine, yin, energy. This is the centre of our sexuality, and also of financial abundance. Where in the root chakra we ground ourselves, here we centre ourselves to find balance between giving and receiving, between others and self. Being centred brings a sense of harmony. Where in the first chakra we are focused on survival, here we start sharing what we have with others; the group, the tribe. This chakra's colour is orange. The element of water here links to emotions. Emotions are contagious, so here we have to distinguish between our emotions and others'. It is also important for our own health to guard against picking up and taking on emotions from others.

As the body depends on a sound foundation, so our lives on earth are founded in the family and community in which we grow up. As children, we are naturally more dependent on our parents, family, teachers, spiritual leaders and other members of the community. At this stage we are affected and influenced by the circumstances in which we are raised. Cultural beliefs, attitudes and values are passed on to us by the group; the tribe. Fear and control can be experienced here. The tribe's intention is to keep the tribe strong and cohesive and ensure its traditions continue. As we grow up and become our own individual selves, we start to question this groupthink and develop minds of our own.

The third energy centre: the solar plexus

Stepping into your own power

The third chakra is located in the solar plexus, just above the navel and below the ribcage. Its colour is yellow – this is the sun inside of us. At this level you become aware of your sense of identity; your unique personality. It is the centre of your personal power, confidence and self-esteem. The element is fire. This is the fire we utilize when we start something new – our enthusiasm, motivation and inner power. This is where we experience anger, although anger is an essential boundary energy and in the positive is great for assertiveness. Here we come into our own right. This is a centre of transformation, as the yang or masculine energy of the fire burns off the excess emotions of the yin sacral chakra. When this energy centre is strong and healthy, you are in touch with your inner power, enthusiasm and spontaneity. You have the confidence to make decisions and be your own, individual self.

With maturity you begin to perceive yourself as an individual, separate from the family or tribe. The psychologist Carl Jung calls this the process of individuating. Breaking away from the tribe is essential for self-discovery. Here you begin to develop a healthy ego, your own opinions and personal power. You also learn to exert this personal power to stand your ground, value your uniqueness and develop confidence and healthy self-esteem. Your willpower motivates you to visualize your desired future, and you use this power to manifest your dreams in life.

The fourth energy centre: the heart chakra

Unconditional love

The heart chakra is in the centre of our bodies; the middle of our physical and spiritual centres. It unites Heaven and Earth. Here we begin to move beyond the ego self, from personal to universal. Here we start our spiritual journey by cultivating compassion and unconditional love – these are the qualities of the heart. Divine love seeks nothing in return. The heart chakra's colour is green and represents harmony and balance. Its element is air, as the heart-centre links to the lungs. Sadness and grief can affect the lungs. Air can be gentle or stormy as it brings change – transforming anger into love, forgiveness and compassion. This centre also promotes self-love which is a powerful healer. Self-love is the foundation of good health and happiness. It is on the basis of self-love that we can reach out to others in love.

The heart chakra is also linked to the hands with which we reach out to touch, love and heal others.

As you begin to move beyond yourself and reach out to others in a selfless way, you live your purpose unconditionally and regardless of rewards. You act in love and are motivated by meaning.

The fifth energy centre: the throat chakra

Speaking your truth

The throat chakra is our centre of communication, self-expression and sound. This is the chakra that builds a bridge between us and the world around us. Throat and thyroid issues may be a result of not expressing yourself. So here we find our voice. The fifth chakra's elements are aether and sound. Aether is space, a blank canvas allowing you to express yourself creatively and freely in this world. This chakra, which is sky blue in colour, opens you up to a higher truth. Being true to yourself, therefore implies honest expression, allowing yourself to communicate your own higher truth.

LIFTING THE VEILS OF ILLUSION

The sixth energy centre: the third eye
Developing intuition and psychic abilities
The sixth chakra is between and slightly above the eyebrows; this is the position of your third eye. Its colour is indigo. This is the centre of our psychic abilities. It promotes inner vision, intuition, concentration and insight. The third eye is closely associated with the pineal gland, a tiny cone-shaped gland sometimes called 'the seat of the soul', believed to be the place where spirit connects with the body. You can promote your inner vision through meditation. Through meditation you energise and maximise the light within. As you meditate on the light ask for inner vision, to be able to perceive the truth, to see the world as it really is – all energy and pure potentiality.

The seventh energy centre: the crown chakra
Spiritual oneness
The crown chakra energizes the upper brain. It has the function of promoting positive thought patterns, inspiration and imagination. This chakra is in charge of spiritual well-being and connects you with your higher self and the cosmic forces. It constantly channels life force energy into your system, aligning and balancing all your chakras. Connecting with the beyond, you experience unity of all things. Having completed the path through the chakras and merged with your true higher self, enlightenment ensues.

Spiritual Laws	Chakra & Glands	Qualities	Meditation & Element	Crystal
Live in the present moment	Crown chakra gland: pituitary	Higher consciousness, spiritual intelligence, enlightenment, bliss, transcendence, awareness	I am Element: thought	Amethyst Clear quartz Selenite
Seek only the truth	Brow/ third eye chakra gland: pineal	Inner vision, intuition, wisdom, psychic perception	I see Element: light	Lapis lazuli Sodalite
Surrender personal will to divine will	Throat chakra gland: thyroid	Communication, expression (of ideas and feelings), higher will, truth	I speak Element: sound, aether (space)	Blue lace agate Turquoise Aquamarine
Love is divine power	Heart chakra gland: thymus	Love, compassion, acceptance, peace, caring, healing through forgiveness	I love Element: air	Peridot Malachite Rose Quartz Green Jade Green aventurine
Honour oneself	Solar plexus glands: adrenals/ pancreas	Personal power, healthy ego, self-worth, passion, freedom of choice, individuality, self-esteem, boundaries, immunity, digestion	I can Element: fire	Citrine Tiger eye Yellow calcite Topaz

Honour one another	Sacral chakra glands: testes and ovaries	Sexuality, emotions, moving forward, material abundance, connection, pleasure, procreation, appetite, life purpose, creativity	I feel Element: water	Carnelian Amber Orange calcite
All is one	Root chakra glands: adrenals	Survival instincts, sense of belonging, group think, culture, safety, security, health, grounding, fear of abandonment	I have Element: earth	Garnet Ruby Red jasper Bloodstone Obsidian Hematite Smoky quartz

Visit _http://liftingtheveilsofillusion.co.uk/meditations/_ to download a free audio meditation: _A Meditative Healing Journey through the Chakras._

Appendix 3

The Stages of Spiritual Growth

Inspired by and adapted from Michael Bernard Beckwith's *The Life Visioning Process.*

At the effect

Our earthly home is a place of duality where we experience many opposites as part of the learning process. The duality can be described as yin and yang, masculine and feminine, light and dark, good and evil, right and wrong and cause and effect. Cause and effect is a universal law and also represents two different levels of consciousness. Do you perceive yourself as mostly at the effect side of life and therefore powerless to do something about your circumstances, or are you mostly operating at the cause side of life, consciously aware of how you cause the things happening in your life and thereby empowered to take action? For as long as you feel affected by influences outside of you, as long as you are finding reasons and excuses for what's happening in your life, you are practically spiritually asleep. Consciously or unconsciously, you perceive yourself as a powerless victim of circumstances. By complaining, blaming, pointing fingers or finding fault, you give your power away and put yourself in the position of the helpless victim. It is a level of awareness focused on the tangible, three-dimensional world of form.

Take responsibility

The only way out of victimhood is to take full responsibility for everything in your life. By taking full responsibility, you fully empower yourself. This insight into the consequences of your beliefs, values, perceptions and actions is the first stage of spiritual awakening.

Manifest magically

Blame must make way for empowerment. Negative and helpless thinking must make way for positive and empowering thoughts. When you are empowered and focused on positive thoughts, you discover the power of your mind and the will to create your life the way you want it. You learn to unleash your inner power, potential and strength to bring about your desired outcomes. You have a vision of your future and a plan to work towards it. You are aware of the vibration of your own energy, the law of attraction and your involvement in the process of manifestation. Your world becomes more fourth dimensional. You utilize your mind and emotions to access the world of energy and potentiality. You know that the third-dimensional world of form and effect can be changed; that you can heal your past and create your own future. You use your creative energy and manifest magically. This is the second stage of spiritual awakening.

Become a channel

At this stage, you become disillusioned by the material world and begin to feel that there must be more to life than this. You are aware that you are spirit in a material world and that there is a higher purpose. You feel ready to yield personal power to a higher power. You become a more receptive channel of something beyond you that you allow to flow through you. You live more in the moment as you are divinely guided in every moment on your path. You become more sensitized to your unique purpose and to a higher purpose that you want to be a part of. You want to help others and contribute to making the world a better place. You become a channel of the divine power. Something magical is happening through you. This is the third stage awakening.

Be the divine

The more you grow and merge your purpose with a higher purpose, the more you become one with this higher intelligence. Now you realize that not only can you channel this higher intelligence, but also, you are this higher intelligence. At this stage you and this higher power become one. You don't just experience the divine within – you are the divine. You are all-powerful yet humble. This is the fourth stage of awakening. You are a fifth-dimensional being. You feel at peace regardless of circumstances.

Appendix 4

What It Means to Be a Light Worker

If you are a light worker, you chose to be here on earth at this time to assist. Light workers have a mission of selfless service. All of us came to the earth plane through the veil of forgetfulness. This happens to level the playing field because many light workers are highly evolved beings. Anyone who chooses the light is a light worker. When you choose the light, you are guided to where and how you can serve best.

Signs

Many light workers choose a challenging childhood to serve as a boot camp. Most of their younger years are preparatory. They can take longer to mature and deepen into their true roles. This is because they have so much more to deepen into. They often feel the odd one out and that they don't fit in. Their inner strength sustains them. They are non-conformists. They often feel different, lonely, isolated and restless. Many have learning difficulties simply because they *are* different and therefore learn differently. The educational system is not always flexible enough to accommodate them. Despite this they can excel academically. They are more spiritual than religious, and yearn for the truth. Vivid dreams are part of their nightly lessons. As a result of their gift of intuition, they are highly sensitive energetically and emotionally. They often experience illness, bodily discomfort and addictions when the path gets tough. Until they wake up to who they are, they can experience self-doubt and feelings of insecurity.

Focus

They need to purify to prepare themselves energetically. Purification raises the level at which their energy vibrates and will allow them to awaken spiritually and to their true role. They need to focus the mind through meditation and connection with the higher self. After awakening, they quickly retrieve the knowledge and wisdom already inside them. They may undergo a rapid redo of all their previous evolutionary processes (physical, emotional and mental) to trigger awakening. The higher vibrations of their energy bodies can be felt physically.

Role

Light workers are here to help – not like average human beings but like magicians. When they begin to work magically they are on their spiritual path. With their higher mind activated, they do energy and mental work to help humankind, often through visualization, intention-setting and telepathic healing of people and circumstances. A key role that light workers play in the world is healing family karma. While releasing karma, they also help raise the level of the planet's vibration.

Regression hypnotherapist Dolores Cannon describes the call that the light workers responded to when they came to this planet to assist in a mass awakening of humanity and to prepare humanity for the arrival of the fifth-dimensional earth. She found remarkable common themes through the many people she regressed under hypnosis, and in her book *Three Waves of Volunteers and the New Earth*, she explains how these volunteers came to the planet in three waves of souls, starting in the mid-1950s. These three waves of souls are often called the Indigo, Crystal and Rainbow Children.

Light workers are the essential link between the spirit world and the physical world and move between dimensions to do their work. This can affect their bodies. Building confidence will help them immensely to follow through on their intuitive nudges. Leadership development is essential.

Be the leader that you are and shine your light brightly in the darkness where it shows up best.

You are here to usher in the new era, the new fifth-dimensional earth. The time is NOW.

Resource List

Contact the author:

Narina Riskowitz
Transformational Coach and Therapist
Bright Future Now
Tel: (+44) 07986 584573
narina@brightfuturenow.co.uk
www.brightfuturenow.co.uk
www.liftingtheveilsofillusion.co.uk

The Performance Partnership
5 Crane Mews
32 Gould Road
Twickenham
Greater London
TW2 6RS
Tel: 020 8992 9523
www.performancepartnership.com

The HeartMath Institute
https://www.heartmath.org
http://www.heartmath.com

Others
http://www.chopra.com
http://www.nature.com
http://www.decoz.com/
http://www.drwaynedyer.com/

Beck, M., 2008. *Steering by Starlight: How to Fulfil Your Destiny No Matter What.*

Benedict, G., 2008. *The Mayan Prophecies for 2012.*

Bernard Beckwith, M., 2008. *The Life Visioning Process: A Evolutionary Journey to Live as Divine Love,* Audio CD.

Byrne, R., 2006. *The Secret.*

Byrne, R., 2010. *The Power.*

Campbell, F., 1931. *Your Days are Numbered, a Manual of Numerology for Everyone.*

Cannon, D., 2011. *The Three Waves of Volunteers and the New Earth.*

Chia, M. and Li, J., 1996. *The Inner Structure of Tai Chi: Tai Chi Chi Kung 1.*

Chopra, D., 1989. *Quantum Healing: Exploring the Frontiers of Mind/Body Medicine.*

Chopra, D., 1994. *The Seven Spiritual Laws of Success: A Practical Guide to the Fulfilment of Your Dreams.*

Chopra, D., 2003. *Synchrodestiny: Harnessing the Infinite Power of Coincidence to Create Miracles.*

Cooper, D. and Crosswell, K., 2010. *The Keys to the Universe: Accessing the Ancient Secrets by Tuning to the Power and Wisdom of the Cosmos.*

Cooper, D., 2000. *A Little Light on the Spiritual Laws.*

Cooper, D., 2009. *2012 and Beyond: An Invitation to Meat the Challenges and Opportunities Ahead.*

Dilts, R., 1990. *Beliefs: Pathways to Health and Well-being.*

Dupree, U. E., 2012. *Ho'oponopono: the Hawaiian Forgiveness Ritual as the Key to Your Life's Fulfilment.*

Dyer, W. D and Chopra, D., 200. *How To Get What You Really, Really, Really, Really Want,* Audio CD.

Dyer, W. D., 1989. *You'll See It When You Believe It: The Way To Your Personal Transformation.*

Eden, D., 1998. *Energy Medicine.*

Edwards, G., 2010. *Conscious Medicine: Creating Health and Well-being in a Conscious Universe.*

Ford, D., 1998. *The Dark Side of the Light Chasers: Reclaiming Your Power, Creativity, Brilliance and Dreams.*

Foundation for Inner Peace, 1992. *A Course in Miracles.*

Freedom Long, M., 1953. *The Secret Science At Work: New Light On Prayer.*

Hanson, R., 2009. *Buddha's Brain: The Practical Neuroscience of Happiness, Love and Wisdom.*

Hawkins, D. R., 1995. *Power vs. Force: The Hidden Determinants of Human Behavior.*

Hay, L., 1984. *You Can Heal Your Life.*

Heaversedge, J. and Halliwell, E., 2010. *The Mindfulness Manifesto: How Doing Less and Noticing More Can Help Us Thrive in a Stressed-out World.*

James, T. and Woodsmall, W., 1988. *Time Line Therapy and the Basis of Personality.*

James, T., 2000. *Hypnosis: A Comprehensive Guide.*

Judith, A., 2004. *Chakras: Wheels of Life.*

Kornfield, J., 2002. *A Path with Heart: The Classical Guide Through the Perils and Promises of Spiritual Life.*

Lipton, B. H., 2005. *The Biology of Belief: Unleashing the Power of Consciousness, Matter and Miracles.*

March, M.D. and McEvans, J., 1976. *The Only Way to Learn Astrology, Vol 1.*

Millman, D., 1993. *The Life You were Born to Live, a Guide to Finding your Life Purpose.*

Myss, C., 1996. *Anatomy of the Spirit: The Seven Stages of Power and Healing.*

Ngan, N. D., 2013. *Your Soul Contract Decoded: Discovering the Spiritual Map of your Life with Numerology.*

Ober, C., Sinatra, S.T. and Zucker, M. 2010. *Earthing: The Most Important Health Discovery Ever?*

Orion, D., 2007. *Astrology for Dummies.*

Parker, J. & D.,1991. *Parkers' Astrology: The Definitive Guide to Using Astrology in Every Aspect of Your Life.*

Ready, R. and Burton, K., 2004. *Neuro-linguistic Programming for Dummies.*

Rinpoche, T. W., 2002. *Healing with Form, Energy and Light: The Five Elements in Tibetan Shamanism, Tantra and Dzogchen.*

Schwartz, R., 2012. *Your Soul's Gift: The Healing Power of the Life you Planned Before you were Born.*

Snowden, R., 2006. *Jung – The Key Ideas.*

Steiner, D., 1995. *Essential Reiki: A Complete Guide to an Ancient Healing Art.*

Talbot, M., 1991. *The Holographic Universe.*

Thomas, C., 1998. *The Journey Home.*

Thomas, C., 1999. *The Fool's First Steps: The True Nature of Reality.*

Thomas, C., and Baker, D., 1999. *Everything You Always Wanted to Know About Your Body But So Far Nobody's Been Able to Tell You.*

Thompson, C., 2013. *Mindfulness and the Natural World: Bringing our Awareness Back to Nature.*

Tirtha, S. S., 1998. The *Ayurveda Encyclopedia: Natural Secrets to Healing, Prevention and Longevity.*

Tolle, E., 2005. *A New Earth: Awakening to Your Life's Purpose.*

Weiss, B.,1988. *Many Lives, Many Masters: The True Story of a Prominent Psychiatrist, His Young Patient and the Past-Life Therapy That Changed Both Their Lives.*

Williamson, M., 1992. *A Return to Love: Reflections on the Principles of A Course in Miracles.*

About the Author

Narina Riskowitz is an experienced transformational therapist and soul coach. She runs spiritual workshops, embraces energy healing and works holistically with individual clients. She has developed a healing modality, combining regression journeys with energy healing for complete results. As she is a firm believer in the mind-body link, most of her work is aimed at releasing negative emotions and limiting beliefs to restore her clients' natural health and inherent confidence. Her ground-breaking course material resulted in her signature soul-coaching tool, *Lifting the Veils of Illusion,* which is now captured in this soul-enriching book.

Originally from South Africa, Narina moved to England with her husband, Calvin Riskowitz, in 2002. She lives and works in Lancashire, Northwest England.

Narina can be contacted by email:
narina@brightfuturenow.co.uk

Her websites:
www.brightfuturenow.co.uk
www.liftingtheveilsofillusion.co.uk

Lightning Source UK Ltd.
Milton Keynes UK
UKOW06f1802090216

268045UK00002B/6/P